THE ARTIST'S FRIENDLY LEGAL GUIDE

THE ARTIST'S FRIENDLY LEGAL GUIDE

Floyd Conner

Roger Gilcrest

Peter Karlen

Jean Perwin

David Spatt

NORTH LIGHT BOOKS Cincinnati, Ohio

The Artist's Friendly Legal Guide. Published by North Light Books, an imprint of F&W Publications, 1507 Dana Avenue, Cincinnati, Ohio 45207.

Manufactured in the United States.

93 92 91 90 89 88   5 4 3 2 1

Library of Congress Cataloging-in-Publication Data

The Artist's friendly legal guide.

   Includes index.
   1. Artists' contracts—United States. 2. Copyright—Art—United States. 3. Copyright—Moral rights—United States. 4. Artists—Taxation—Law and legislation—United States. I. Conner, Floyd, 1951-
KF390.A7A785   1988   346.7304'82   88-25478
ISBN 0-89134-256-7   347.306482

Editor: Susan Conner
Designer: Carol Buchanan

CONTENTS

INTRODUCTION

Whether you're a painter, illustrator, designer, or cartoonist, it's important for you to know about basic legal issues. This book will help you understand everything you need to know about copyright, contracts, moral rights, taxes, and recordkeeping.

It's likely that you have already encountered these issues without understanding the part you play in them. Perhaps you have signed contracts without knowing what you've agreed to, or you may have accepted a work-for-hire assignment without being aware of everything it entails. It's time that you understand the legal aspects of your business so that you will be on equal footing with the businesspersons you deal with.

The purpose of this book is to explain seemingly complicated issues in simple, friendly terms. Since this is not a legal manual, we cannot address all the intricacies of every legal problem and therefore advise you to seek the help of an attorney if a serious problem arises. But after reading this book, you will understand the fundamentals of legal issues you encounter every day and be able to deal effectively with them.

Chapter 1, "Copyright Law," spells out what you can do to protect the rights to your work and how you can prevent others from copying it. It also tells you how to register your copyright. We've included an example of a registration form to illustrate the step-by-step instructions provided in the chapter. We've also given you information on what works fall into public domain and what qualifies as *fair use* so you'll know how and when you can use other artists' works.

Another special feature is the section on the use of computer artwork. Computers have expanded artistic techniques and styles, but they have also raised questions about copy-

right—when computer artists use the computer to enhance another's work, are they merely copying work or are they creating original works of art? You'll find an answer to this question, as well as an agreement for use of computer artwork, in this chapter.

Sample agreements presented in the chapter on contracts feature easy-to-understand terminology that you can adapt to fit your needs. There's a contract for almost any situation—gallery representation, illustration of a magazine or a book, syndication, graphic design—plus a model release form.

You're faced with taxes every year; the chapter covering taxes and recordkeeping will ease your fears the next time around. We'll outline good bookkeeping habits so you can face next year's returns with confidence. Since many of you are self-employed, we offer advice on what forms to fill out and when to file them. We also give advice for those of you who are pursuing art as a hobby or as a part-time occupation, and a run-down on deductions, including the home office deduction.

Artists in the United States are catching up with those in Europe in gaining more control over their work. The controversial topics of moral rights and ethical business practices are covered in a chapter that explains what rights are available to you and how to avoid business practices that can hurt you.

The attorneys who have contributed to this book realize the problems artists face. As members of various Volunteer Lawyers for the Arts organizations, they have learned first-hand that artists urgently need help to protect their creative rights and conduct successful art businesses. They wrote this book so that you can apply some preventive medicine to your business practices now and avoid costly mistakes later.

CHAPTER 1
COPYRIGHT LAW

COPYRIGHT AND THE ARTIST: AN OVERVIEW

by Peter H. Karlen

Copyrights are the lifeblood for many artists. After all, when you have a copyright in a work, you can control the work and profit from its commercial use. Therefore, as a fine or graphic artist, you must have a good understanding of copyright law if you want to make the most of your career.

The purpose of this chapter is to outline copyright law. A full discussion of copyright law would take hundreds of pages, but this brief discussion gives you enough information to understand copyright law and begin protecting your rights.

THE PURPOSES OF COPYRIGHT

Your copyright gives you a monopoly on your work. Without it, anyone could copy your work and use it for any purpose without any payment to you. With a copyright, you have the exclusive right to commercially exploit the work.

The principal purpose of copyright law,

Peter H. Karlen practices art, literary, and entertainment law, including the law of copyrights, trademarks, and nonprofit organizations, in La Jolla, California. He has taught art law and intellectual property law courses for a number of years in law schools in Britain and the United States. In addition, Mr. Karlen is a contributing editor to Artweek *and has written numerous articles on art law for other art and legal publications. He holds a J.D. from the University of California, Hastings College of the Law; and an M.S. (Law & Society) from the University of Denver College of Law. He is also director of the San Diego Lawyers for the Arts.*

however, is not to protect artists, writers, and other creative persons, or even to protect their publishers, but rather to promote the arts and other creative activities. The *United States Constitution* gives Congress the right to enact patent and copyright laws in order to:

> promote the Progress of Science and Useful Arts, by securing for limited Times to Authors and Inventors the exclusive Right to their respective Writings and Discoveries.

Artists, writers, and their publishers own copyrights, but it is society that ultimately benefits from protection for individuals. After all, if creative persons and their publishers were not given exclusive rights to publish their works, artists and especially writers would be discouraged from producing works because anyone else could copy and profit from them. Also, publishers would not invest money in publishing works that could be immediately pirated by rivals. The theory is that giving exclusive publication rights to creative persons will encourage them and their publishers to produce more works.

THE RIGHTS GRANTED BY COPYRIGHT

A copyright gives the owner five exclusive rights. These are the exclusive rights to reproduce, adapt, publicly distribute copies of, publicly display, and publicly perform the copyrighted work.

If anyone else exercises one of these exclusive rights without authorization, that person is considered an *infringer* and is liable to the owner.

Let's look at each of the five exclusive rights. The exclusive right to *reproduce* the work gives artists the right to make copies of their works in any medium of expression. For instance, your copyright in a cartoon character gives you the exclusive right to reproduce it in any form, from posters to greeting cards.

The exclusive right to *adapt* the work means you can prepare derivative works based on the original work. By statute a *derivative work* is:

> A work based upon one or more pre-existing works, such as a translation, musical arrangement, dramatization, fictionalization, motion picture version, sound recording, art reproduction, abridgement, condensation, or any other form in which a work may be recast, transformed, or adapted. A work consisting of editorial revisions, annotations, elaborations, or other modifications which, as a whole, represent an original work of authorship, is a 'derivative work'.

Thus the exclusive right to adapt a line drawing extends to the right to turn that drawing into a painting or sculpture. (This right is not covered by the right to reproduce because it entails more than simply making physical copies of the original.)

The exclusive *distribution* right gives the copyright owner the right to publicly sell, lend, lease, and otherwise distribute copies of the work. Therefore, only the owner has the right to send out copies of the work to buyers, critics, and publishers. (There are some exceptions to this right, which we'll discuss later.)

The exclusive *performance* right, which doesn't usually apply to visual art, is the right to publicly perform the work by acting it or reciting it (in the case of literary works) or by exhibiting it (in the case of motion picture films).

The exclusive *display* right is just that, the right to display the work publicly at an art gallery or any other place open to the public.

Limitations on the Exclusive Rights

For good reasons, these exclusive rights are limited. Copyright law doesn't permit artists to monopolize the world of utilitarian objects merely by drawing them. Just because you draw a car, an airplane, or a can opener doesn't mean you can use copyright law to stop people from manufacturing them.

Similarly, if your drawing is reproduced in a useful article sold to the public, you can't use your copyright in the drawing to prevent others from making, distributing, and displaying pictures or photographs of these articles in advertisements, news reports, or commentaries related to the sale of the articles. For example, if your artwork were reproduced on a T-shirt, retailers selling the shirts could use photographs of the shirts in advertisements even though the photographs depicted your artwork. The law says artists' rights must be subordinate to the interests of manufacturers, distributors, and the news media in advertising and commenting upon products sold to the public.

Distribution and display rights are also restricted by common sense. If you sell a copy of your work, the purchaser has the right to display and resell that copy despite your exclusive rights of public display and distribution. If the legitimate owner of an art object could not display or resell it because of the artist's rights, then few people would ever buy paintings, drawings, or other works of art.

WHAT CAN BE COPYRIGHTED?

The Copyright Act defines material that can be copyrighted as "original works of authorship fixed in any tangible medium of expression, now known or later developed, from which they can be perceived, reproduced, or otherwise communicated, either directly or with the aid of a machine or device . . ." The key words here are *original*, *work of authorship*, and *fixed*.

Originality

Only *original* works are protected. This doesn't mean that the work has to be novel—that it never existed in the past in any form. All that's necessary is that you created something original, without copying or plagiarizing. Thus, the work must spring from your own creative efforts. If someone else independently created the very same work, that is of no consequence, and you still have a copyright.

This doesn't mean the work must be totally original. An artist can take an older work and embellish it. His new work will be considered a *derivative work*, and his protection will extend only to the part of the work that is *original* with him and not to the pre-existing part of the work. Naturally, if another person owned a copyright in the pre-existing work and the artist prepared a derivative work without permission, he would be a copyright infringer, but this wouldn't affect his copyright in the part of the new work that he alone created. On the other hand, if no one holds a copyright in the pre-existing work, it would fall into what's known as the *public domain*. The artist then would *not* be a copyright infringer and would own a copyright on his portion of the work without having any claim to the pre-existing work.

Authorship

To gain protection, you must create a *work of authorship*. For purposes of illustration, works of authorship are classified as follows:

- Literary works
- Musical works, including any accompanying words
- Dramatic works, including any accompanying music
- Pantomimes and choreographic works
- Pictorial, graphic, and sculptural works
- Motion pictures and other audiovisual works
- Sound recordings

To be considered a work of authorship, your artwork must show some minimal amount of creativity. Thus, a drawing of a circle or square usually will not be protected; minimal art will have some problems as well. A writer who submits a word or title won't be able to claim protection for a literary work. In the graphic arts field, other creative output usually not protected includes layout, calligraphy, typeface design, and blank forms. Arrangements of color, if sufficiently original, are protectable; so are maps, technical drawings such as architectural drawings, diagrams, photographs, prints, art reproductions, globes, charts, models, and even labels affixed to merchandise if they have sufficient artistic content.

You might ask, what is so "original" and "creative" about a map? Even though the roads and terrain are well known and in the public domain, the cartographer exercises his own creativity in choosing colors, symbols, roads, place names, and other elements of the map.

Don't despair if the Copyright Office rejects your claim to copyright in a chart, work of calligraphy, or other type of work that is not usually protected. If there is sufficient creative content and originality, you can sometimes persuade the Copyright Office examiner to accept your claim.

The Copyright Office does not examine how the artist actually arrived at the result—only the results count. For example, the artist who creates a drawing using a computer can claim protection if the result has a certain amount of complexity and artistic content. The same is true even of the artist who dips worms in paint or ink and lets them crawl all over a canvas. A poet who takes words out of a hat and randomly creates poetry may also claim protection.

Fixation

To have protection there must be *fixation*; in other words, your work must be "put on paper." Copyright law does not protect works that exist merely in the imagination. For example, if you develop in your mind the artwork for an advertisement and disclose the concept to an advertising agency, you can't properly sue the advertising agency for copyright infringement if it steals your work. When the work is put on paper, recorded on a phonorecord, entered into a computer's memory, or otherwise can be perceived, reproduced, or communicated on or from a tangible medium, then copyright protection applies.

WHAT CAN'T BE COPYRIGHTED

Important subject matter outside the scope of copyright protection includes ideas and utilitarian works.

Ideas

The Copyright Act says that ideas, systems, methods of operation, discoveries, and the like are not protected no matter what form they take or how they are described in the copyrightable work. The architect who draws architectural designs incorporating new concepts can't stop others from stealing the concepts so long as they don't steal the drawings themselves. The person who writes a new business plan and secures a copyright for the text can't use copyright law to stop others from going into business using the plan.

To protect an idea, you must, for example, use the law of contracts or the law of confidential relationships, as discussed on page 34.

Utilitarian Works

Protection is also limited if the work is utilitarian. "Works of artistic craftsmanship" are protectable insofar as their form but not their mechanical or utilitarian aspects are concerned. For instance, if you design a lamp base in the form of a figurative sculpture, you can get a copyright in the sculptural work, but you can't use copyright law to keep other people from making lamps.

The copyright law also says:

> [T]he design of a useful article . . . shall be considered a pictorial, graphic, or sculptural work only if, and only to the extent that, such design incorporates pictorial, graphic, or sculptural features that can be identified separately from, and are capable of existing independently of, the utilitarian aspects of the article.

For example, clothing designers cannot get copyright protection for most aspects of their designs because clothing consists of utilitarian articles intended to cover the body. However, if an item of clothing has frills that aren't merely there to clothe the body but exist only as ornaments, separate copyright protection can apply to these elements. The same is true of buildings. These architectural works are clearly utilitarian, but if there are unusual façades or reliefs on the buildings, they may be separately protected as sculptural works.

One reason why copyright law does not fully extend to utilitarian works is that it would conflict with the purposes of patent law. Patent laws give protection to utilitarian inventions, such as machines and processes, in order to reward inventors but at the same time let the inventions fall into the public domain after short periods of time. If these inventions enjoyed the lengthy terms of copyright protection, the public wouldn't have access to them for unduly long periods of time.

U.S. Government Works

U.S. government works, including reports, transcripts, surveys, and maps, also don't enjoy copyright protection. However, this only applies to works created by U.S. government officers and employees and not to copyrights transferred or bequeathed to the United States government. Maybe the reason is to give citizens complete access to government works. After all, government works are created with taxpayers' money.

This doesn't mean that you can copy everything the government creates. Try making actual copies of U.S. currency or postage stamps, and see the consequences. The government can protect itself using other laws, such as criminal statutes that penalize forgery and tampering with U.S. currency.

Technically there is nothing to prevent a state government from holding copyrights in works created by its employees—or its citizens. As a practical matter, however, state governments seldom enforce their copyrights against citizens. Four states (Florida, California, Virginia, and Michigan) have granted copyright immunity to state agencies such as universities; this allows the agencies to use creative work without permission. Artists are now challenging these dangerous precedents.

Obscene, Libelous, Seditious, and Fraudulent Works

There used to be controversies about whether obscene, libelous, fraudulent, and seditious works could be copyrighted. Even though a few old court decisions say that obscene works are not copyrightable, as a practical matter, sexually explicit, deceitful, revolutionary, and defamatory works are copyrightable. The Copyright Office is not about to embroil itself in First Amendment controversies.

OWNERSHIP

Generally speaking, the copyright owner of a work is the person who created it. However, not everyone is eligible for copyright protection, nor are individual creators of works necessarily their owners.

Publication and Nationality

The copyright laws allow anyone to own copyrights in unpublished works, but there are restrictions on published works. For example, U.S. citizens and persons living in the United States can own copyrights under U.S. law in published works. Foreign nationals can own U.S. copyrights in works first published in the United States. In addition, residents of countries that have copyright treaties with the United States, "stateless" persons, and persons given protection by presidential decree are eligible for protection. All other persons, including other foreign nationals, are not given U.S. protection for published works.

However, foreigners can secure U.S. copyright protection by publishing their works with a proper three-element copyright notice according to the terms of the Universal Copyright Convention, a treaty to which the United States is a party.

Joint Authorship and Ownership

Usually, if you create a work alone, you will be the copyright owner. But what if you work with someone else? Your collaboration could yield a "joint work" owned by both of you.

To have a joint work, there must be a mutual intention to collaborate. Joint authorship cannot be forced. If you have created a work and someone wants to add to it against your will, that person cannot unilaterally create a joint work.

When there is mutual intention, each contribution may either be *interdependent* or *inseparable*. For example, if two people paint a painting together so that their contributions cannot be readily separated or isolated, then they have created inseparable contributions. However, if two artists work on a painting that consists of several panels, each artist working on different panels, then the contributions are interdependent. In both cases, the works reflect joint authorship.

Nonetheless, not every contribution makes someone a joint author. The contribution must be more than minimal. The printer who merely whites out some smudges and stray marks on your artwork won't be a joint author of the work. Nor does a foundry worker become the joint author of a sculpture merely because he pours molten metal into a mold.

On the other hand, just because a contribution standing by itself would not be copyrightable doesn't mean it won't be a qualifying contribution. For instance, a person who contributes ideas and suggestions toward a painting, book, or play may be considered a joint author if her contributions are significant even if that person never touches a brush or pen.

Other Means of Creating Joint Ownership When joint authors create a work together, they become the joint copyright *owners* of the work. Joint ownership is also created when a single owner transfers a fractional part or parts of a copyright to someone else or transfers the entire copyright to two or more persons. For instance, if a sole owner transfers a copyright to five other people, those five people all become joint copyright owners of the work.

Consequences of Joint Ownership The consequences of joint ownership are as follows: First, unless there is a contrary written agreement, all joint owners are equal owners regardless of the extent of their contributions. For instance, if one person contributes ten percent of a drawing or ten percent of a text while the other person contributes the remaining ninety percent, each will still have equal ownership. The law won't apportion ownership according to the respective contributions of the parties because doing so would require judges to determine not only the quantity of the respective contributions but also their quality. Unlike joint ownership of real property, when one joint owner dies, his ownership interest goes to his heirs, not to the other joint owner.

Also, even if the contributions are interdependent, one joint author can't sell off the rights to his own contribution without the consent of the other joint author, and he can't license his contribution without accounting for profits to the other joint author. For example, if one person creates the pictorial elements of a map and the other person contributes the text, both artist and writer own one-half interests in the entire work, and the artist can't sell off the artwork by itself without the consent of the writer or license the artwork by itself without accounting to the writer for his share of the profits.

Any joint owner can grant a nonexclusive license to use the work without the consent of the others. But if the owner granting the license receives money for this grant, he must pay the other joint owners their shares of the net profits. For instance, if a joint owner owning one-third of the copyright received $1,500 from licensing, that owner would have to pay $1,000 to the other joint owners.

However, no joint owner can grant an exclusive license or transfer the copyright without the consent of the other joint owners.

One more thing, community property laws complicate joint ownership. If you reside in a community property state, your spouse may have ownership interests in your copyrights even if he or she did not contribute to the works, unless you have a contrary written agreement. Consult a lawyer about marital property laws as they affect your copyrights, especially if you contemplate writing a will or filing for a divorce.

WORKS MADE FOR HIRE

One category of artwork that can't be copyrighted by the artist, even though it meets the criteria of being an "original work of authorship fixed in any tangible medium," is work that has been made for hire.

When a work is considered a *work made for hire*, then the employer who commissioned it is not only the owner but also the "author." It's almost as if the creative person, the employee or independent contractor, didn't exist. You have no say in how the work is reproduced, altered, or displayed and no right to any profits made.

Since creating a work made for hire means you lose virtually all your rights in the work, if you want to reserve any rights, then do so in writing. For instance, you may want to reserve the right to publicly display the work or reproduce it for your portfolio or other self-promotional activities. (See page 51 for more information on how to protect yourself when making a work made for hire.)

A work made for hire may be created in two ways.

First, every work of authorship created by an employee "within the scope of employment" is considered a work made for hire, unless you have a written agreement saying that it's not.

Second, independent contractors may also create works made for hire if the following three conditions exist:

1. The work is specially ordered or commissioned;
2. There is a written "work-for-hire"

agreement; and

3. The work is for use as a contribution to a collective work, a part of a motion picture or other audiovisual work, a supplementary work, a compilation, an instructional text, a test, answer material for a test, or an atlas.

Works Created by Employees

To claim that an employee's work was made for hire, the employer must prove not only that the artist was a true "employee" but also that the work was created "within the scope of employment." The employer need not show that the employee had a full-time job or that the employee was paid a regular salary. However, the employer must establish that he had some right to control or supervise the work of the employee. Other indications of the employment relationship are payroll deductions, W-2 forms, the employee's use of the employer's office space and equipment, and the employee's having a job title.

To prove that the work was created within the scope of employment, the employer merely shows that creating the work was within the responsibilities of the employee according to the employee's job description, or else that the employee was instructed to produce the work.

If the employee creates the work on his own time without compensation and without supervision of the employer, there may not be a work made for hire even if the work relates to the employer's business.

Specially Commissioned Works

In order to claim that a work is commissioned as a work made for hire, the employer must first use a properly drafted "made-for-hire" agreement that mentions that the work is one made for hire. Most important, the work must fall within one of the categories specifically mentioned in the Copyright Act. If the employer specially commissions a work and uses a work-made-for-hire agreement but the work is not within one of the specified categories, there is no work made for hire. (Note that the specified works relate principally to the motion picture and publishing industries, which shows how powerful these industries are in claiming work-made-for-hire protection for employers.)

Of particular concern to the visual artist are the categories "supplementary work" (which includes illustrations for books, as well as maps, charts, and tables) and "collective work." A *collective work* is:

> a work, such as a periodical issue, anthology, or encyclopedia, in which a number of contributions, constituting separate and independent works in themselves, are assembled into a collective whole.

The copyright owner of a collective work, such as an issue of a magazine, is the publisher or other person who compiled the separate contributions.

Just because the publisher owns the copyright in the collective work doesn't mean that he owns the separate contributions. If you contribute to a magazine as an independent contractor without a work-made-for-hire agreement, you will own the copyright in your contribution, and the publisher has only limited rights to use your contribution.

TRANSFERS

Like other personal property, copyrights may be transferred from one owner to another. To transfer a copyright, you must use a *signed*, written document because oral transfers have no legal effect. The lawmakers apparently felt that the ownership of copyrights was too important to be affected by transactions not confirmed in writing. Moreover, the copyright recording system would be nullified if copyrights could be transferred orally.

As far as written documents are concerned, almost anything will do. The document can be a long contract or a short note or memorandum. Sometimes a transfer can be effected even by the writing on the back of a check.

A will also suffices. By will, you can transfer a copyright so that after your death the copyright will pass to the beneficiary(s). If you don't have a will, the copyright will pass to your heirs, as any other personal property would.

Although many informal documents will suffice, I recommend that you have the transferring party execute a certificate of acknowledgment in front of a notary or other person authorized to administer oaths and have that certificate accompany the transfer document. The certificate is not required, but it strengthens the legal effect of the transfer document. Also, you may want to secure more than one signed copy of the transfer document, because original signed copies are more easily recorded, and if you lose the one and only signed copy, you can have problems.

The consequences of a transfer are different from those of a work-for-hire agreement with an employer. With a work made for hire, the employer is the author and doesn't even have to mention your name when registering the copyright. However, with a transfer, you still remain the author, and the new owner is merely the transferee. In any copyright registration, your name should be mentioned as the author, along with the fact that you transferred the copyright. In addition, the artist-copyright owner who transfers the copyright may have the right to terminate the transfer later on, whereas the artist creating a work made for hire usually can't get the copyright back from the employer.

Involuntary "Transfers"

A copyright cannot be taken away from you against your will, because there is no such thing as an involuntary transfer. For instance, if someone sues you and gets the court to enter a judgment against you, the creditor cannot satisfy the judgment by seizing your copyrights. On the other hand, if you commence bankruptcy proceedings, you can lose your copyrights because you voluntarily placed your assets before the court. Also, if you mortgage your copyright, as you would any other property, you can lose the copyright if you default on the loan.

THE COPYRIGHT ACT OF 1909

Before the *Copyright Revision Act of 1976* went into effect on January 1, 1978, federal copyright laws covered all *published* works, that is, all works for which copies had been distributed to the public by rental, lease, lending, sale, or other means. Moreover, there was a parallel system of state statutory and common law protection for unpublished works.

Under this dual system of protection, if a work remained unpublished, it could receive virtually perpetual protection under common law. The author or artist didn't have to register or use copyright notices. However, once a work was published, the owner had to comply with federal statutes requiring copyright notices and other formalities.

The 1976 Copyright Act changed all that. After January 1, 1978, federal copyright law preempted all comparable state statutes and common law rules, at least in all areas regulated by the new federal legislation.

In other words, after January 1, 1978, if the copyright owner tried to protect any of his five exclusive rights for any work covered by the new Copyright Act, then that person had to turn to federal copyright law without any resort to state statutes or common law.

Some areas are not covered by the new law. For example, because unfixed works are excluded from federal copyright protection, you must rely on state statutes or common law to protect a work you've never put down on paper—that is, a work that exists in your imagination only. Also, if someone destroys your work, you can't use federal copyright law as a remedy because the 1976 Copyright Act does not give you the exclusive right to destroy your work.

A good reason for knowing the distinction between state and federal protection is that some of your works may have been created or published before the effective date of the new copyright legislation, and perhaps you may want to know your rights when you copy works by others created and/or published before the effective date of the new legislation.

Works Covered Under the 1909 Act

Under the 1909 Copyright Act, the general

term of protection was only twenty-eight years, but the copyright owner, and in some cases the author, could file an application for renewal during the twenty-eighth year of the first term and secure an additional twenty-eight years of protection, giving a full term of fifty-six years. Failure to file with the Copyright Office during the twenty-eighth year of the first term caused the copyright to be terminated after the first twenty-eight years.

The critical question is, what is the effect of the new legislation on works and copyrights originally subject to state laws and to the 1909 Copyright Act? The general rules are that, works created before the effective date of the new Act (January 1, 1978) and remaining unpublished will be protected under the new Act; similarly, copyrights in published works in their first twenty-eight-year term on January 1, 1978, or in their second twenty-eight-year term within one year of the effective date of the new Act (between December 31, 1976 through December 31, 1977) are covered under the new Act beyond the fifty-six years allowed under the 1909 Act.

Thus, unpublished works created before January 1, 1978, are given the general term of protection under the new Act, which is life of the author plus fifty years or the alternative term for anonymous and pseudonymous works and works made for hire. Interestingly enough, there is an added bonus for such unpublished works: the term of copyrights in these works, no matter what, does not expire before December 31, 2002, and for any such unpublished work that is published before December 31, 2002, the term does not expire before December 31, 2027. This means that, no matter when the author died, and no matter when the work was first created—which could have been hundreds of years ago—the copyright will get a minimum additional term of twenty-five years beyond the effective date of the new Act, and if published during that twenty-five-year period will get another minimum term of twenty-five years.

Thus, if you copy very old unpublished works, you are still at risk. Of course, if the work is very, very old, it's doubtful that there will be heirs who can trace title to the work and pursue you for copyright infringement.

If the work was published under the 1909 Act and subject to a twenty-eight year term, with possibility of renewal, then it will be covered under the new Act but only under the following conditions: If the copyright was in its first twenty-eight year term on January 1, 1978, the copyright will continue to endure for twenty-eight years from the date of first publication with notice. However, if the owner (and sometimes the author) files for a renewal during the twenty-eighth year of the first term, he gets an extension of forty-seven rather than twenty-eight years, for a total term of seventy-five years.

If the copyright is in its second twenty-eight-year renewal term or registered for renewal between December 31, 1976 and December 31, 1977, then it is allowed to extend for a total of seventy-five years from the date of first publication with notice.

This means that you should be careful about filing renewals for any works published under the 1909 Copyright Act during the twenty-eighth year of their first term. Similarly, you can be sure that if no renewal application were filed and registered during the twenty-eighth year for a published work protected under the 1909 Act, then the copyright would expire and you could freely copy the work.

By the way, don't assume that old copyrights renewed for a second twenty-eight-year term under the 1909 Act expired at the end of fifty-six years, even if the fifty-six-year term ended before December 31, 1976. In the early 1960s, special legislation enacted in anticipation of new copyright legislation provided that any copyrights subsisting in their renewal term on September 19, 1962, that were scheduled to expire before December 31, 1976, were extended to that later date.

Most works published under the 1909 Act have their copyrights expire after the first term because most owners and authors don't know about renewal applications.

Remember that the terms of copyrights run to the end of the calendar year in which they would otherwise expire.

On page 25, I set forth a summary concerning the duration of copyright. It should help you to determine how long your works will be protected, but more important, to judge what works you can copy without liability.

This summary is meant only as a guideline, so do not make any judgments about what you can copy without consulting a qualified copyright attorney.

Recording a Transfer

Generally speaking, the first person to receive a transfer is the new owner. However, if the new owner doesn't record the transfer with the Copyright Office and another person takes a later transfer of the very same copyright but records that transfer first, the later transfer may prevail over the first. There is an exception to this rule. The first new owner has a grace period of one month from the date of the transfer to record the transfer, and if he does so within that period, the first transfer will prevail over a second transfer recorded first. Also, to prevail, the second new owner must show that he acted in good faith, not knowing of the first transfer, and for valuable consideration, meaning that the second owner paid for the right to use the work.

To record a transfer with the Copyright Office, send a transfer document bearing the *actual* signature of the original owner or a copy accompanied by a sworn or official certification that it is a true copy of the original signed document. To have a full legal effect, the document or material attached to it must specifically identify the work to which it pertains. That way, after the document is indexed at the Copyright Office, it would be revealed by a reasonable search under the title or registration number for the work. You should also make sure that the original copyright has already been registered.

Dividing a Copyright

A copyright is like a pie that can be carved up in many ways. For instance, you can transfer a certain fraction of the entire copyright, or the copyright can be carved up geographically. As an example, one can transfer North American rights to another person so that person can exclusively exercise rights in North America. The copyright also can be divided by time—for instance, a transfer can be limited to a period of five years—or by medium of expression. One person can receive rights to make photographic reproductions while another receives rights to make silkscreen versions.

Regaining Your Rights

Transfers are not totally irrevocable. For copyright transfers executed by you on or after January 1, 1978, you can terminate the transfer and reacquire your rights during a period of five years beginning at the end of thirty-five years from the date of executing the transfer. You do so by serving the transferee with a written notice of termination specifying a date of termination within the five-year period and by recording this notice with the Copyright Office. The notice is served not more than ten nor less than two years before the date of termination.

The Copyright Act provides a similar method of terminating transfers executed before January 1, 1978, for works covered under the 1909 Copyright Act. For these works, termination may occur any time during a five-year period beginning at the end of fifty-six years from the date of first publication of the work or beginning on January 1, 1978, whichever is later. As with later works, the notice is served neither more than ten nor less than two years before the date of termination and is recorded with the Copyright Office.

These termination rights do not apply to works made for hire. In fact, there are so many exceptions and qualifications to these rights that you really must use the services of an attorney to effect a termination. The purpose here is only to show you that these rights exist.

Distinction Between Art Objects and Copyrights

The law says that owning the copyright is distinct from owning the art object itself:

> Ownership of a copyright, or of any of the exclusive rights under a copyright, is distinct from ownership of any material object in which the work is embodied. Transfer of ownership of any material object, including the copy or phonorecord in which the work is first fixed, does not of itself convey any rights in the copyrighted work embodied in the object; nor, in the absence of an agreement, does transfer of ownership of a copyright or of any exclusive rights under a

copyright convey property rights in any material object.

Thus, by selling a drawing, you do not transfer the copyright unless there is a separate written agreement confirming the transfer. Moreover, by transferring the copyright in the drawing, you do not necessarily transfer the physical drawing itself. Therefore, someone purchasing the physical drawing from you cannot reproduce it without your permission. Similarly, the person who buys the copyright from you does not necessarily have access to the physical drawing, even to reproduce it, unless there is an express or implied understanding that you will permit access.

LICENSES

You can employ several methods to allow others to use your copyrighted work. One method that gives others limited rights to your work without forcing you to give up your copyright is *licensing*.

A copyright license is a permission granted by the copyright owner allowing another person to exercise one or more of the owner's exclusive rights. The person granting the license, usually the owner, is considered the *licensor*, and the person receiving the license is the *licensee*. For example, you could grant someone the right to reproduce your work and display copies of it, or you could license the right to distribute copies without also granting reproduction rights.

Usually licensing agreements are in writing, but that need not be so, as explained below.

Exclusive versus Nonexclusive

The two principal types of licenses are *exclusive* and *nonexclusive*. With an exclusive license, a piece of the copyright is given away, perhaps only for a brief time, in a restricted territory, or for restricted media. No other person, not even the copyright owner, can exercise the rights that have been licensed.

The nonexclusive license permits the copyright owner to give more than one person the same rights. Even the copyright owner can exercise the granted rights. Unlike the exclusive license, it need not be in writing.

A prospective licensee will probably pay a lot more for an exclusive license than for a nonexclusive one since it gives the licensee a monopoly in the area the license covers. Another advantage for the exclusive licensee is that he becomes the owner of the licensed rights and can bring a copyright infringement action on his own. For instance, if you grant an exclusive license to reproduce and distribute your work in Alabama, the licensee can bring a copyright infringement action against anyone else who wrongfully distributes your work in Alabama.

Before you grant a license, carefully consider its scope. If you want to continue exercising rights yourself or license others to do so, you must carefully limit the rights granted. Remember that if you grant a nonexclusive license for certain rights, you can't grant an exclusive license to someone else for those rights because the rights have already been encumbered.

Licensing Considerations

Without going into much detail, here are some considerations for a licensing agreement.

How are you paid? Sometimes a flat lump sum payment will be made; other times, payments will be made in installments. However, more frequently, when both licensor and licensee are taking a chance—where there is no established market for the licensed product, for example—royalties are paid. If so, you should try to determine industry standards for royalties on similar articles. Determine not only the range of acceptable percentages but also the types of proceeds upon which royalties are calculated. For example, if the licensee is manufacturing and selling articles that incorporate your artwork, do you want a percentage of *wholesale* proceeds or *retail* proceeds? Is the percentage of *gross* proceeds or *net* proceeds? If net proceeds, what deductions may the licensee take from gross proceeds to calculate net? Deductions typically include returns, quantity discounts, and amounts received from sales taxes.

Do you want an advance? In other words, do you want an upfront lump sum payment to be applied toward future royalties in order to encourage the licensee to make sales and make up for the advance? Also, do you want the licensee to pay you a *minimum guaranteed royalty* in order to keep the license in effect? If you don't require this, the licensee can keep the license going without making substantial payments.

In addition, you want *fixed accounting periods* for which you will receive timely, accurate, and detailed statements of account. You don't want an accounting once a year; probably you'll ask for monthly accountings but will settle at least for quarterly accountings. Typically, the licensee will then give you a statement of account not more than fifteen, twenty, or thirty days after the end of each calendar quarter, to be accompanied by payment of royalties owed from the immediately preceding calendar quarter.

To ensure payment, you must have the right to *inspect, copy, and audit the licensee's books and records*, and the licensee must keep complete, detailed, and accurate books and records regarding all transactions concerning the license.

How are you credited? Another consideration is credits. To get credits when your artwork is reproduced on licensed articles, you must require them in the agreement. Also, to maintain copyright protection, you must have a clause requiring the licensee to affix a proper copyright notice on all copies of your work.

How do you maintain quality? If your name will be connected with the licensed articles, then you may want them to be of reputable quality. You will need a clause on quality control giving you the right to approve the initial production prototypes and to receive free samples off the production line every few months.

How is the license agreement terminated? You also need detailed provisions on ending the license. Obviously, if the licensee isn't making royalty payments, goes into bankruptcy, or otherwise defaults, you should have the right to terminate the license immediately.

Implied Licenses and Permissions

Licenses can be either *express* or *implied*. An express license is one granted overtly, either orally or in writing. For instance, any license granted in a written licensing agreement is an express license. An implied license occurs when the circumstances of the transaction show an intent to grant a license even though the parties may not have discussed licensing arrangements in so many words. For example, say an artist publishes a pattern book for stained-glass art designs or sewing designs. Even though the book contains no written permission allowing for reproduction of the designs, readers have an implied license because that's what the artist intended.

One type of implied license is even mentioned in the Copyright Act, which talks about contributions to collective works. A writer or artist contributing to a collective work, such as a magazine, obviously expects the publisher to reproduce the contribution in the collective work. However, as the statute says:

> In the absence of an express transfer of the copyright or of any rights under it, the owner of copyright in the collective work is presumed to have acquired only the privilege of that reproducing and distributing the contribution as part of that collective work, any revision of that collective work, and any later collective work in the same series.

In other words, the statute limits any implied license that may have been granted.

HOW TO COPYRIGHT YOUR WORK

Once you've determined that a work can be copyrighted, you may be wondering how you go about getting the copyright. Technically, a copyright exists from the moment the work is "fixed" in a tangible medium of expression.

However, you must do certain things to preserve a copyright. First, when a work is "published," you must use an appropriate copyright notice with it. Second, you often should register the copyright with the Copyright Office at the Library of Congress. If you don't follow these procedures, your work could fall into the public domain.

Copyright Notices

The first step in protecting your copyright is to use notices on all copies of the work upon publication. According to the Copyright Act, *publication* is:

> the distribution of copies or phonorecords of a work to the public by sale or other transfer of ownership, or by rental, lease, or lending. The offering to distribute copies or phonorecords to a group of persons for purposes of further distribution, public performance, or public display, constitutes publication. A public performance or display of a work does not of itself constitute publication.
>
> To perform or display a work "publicly" means—
> (1) to perform or display it at a place open to the public or at any place where a substantial number of persons outside of a normal circle of a family and its social acquaintances is gathered; or
> (2) to transmit or otherwise communicate a performance or display of the work to a place specified by clause (1) or to the public, by means of any device or process, whether the members of the public capable of receiving the performance or display receive it in the same place or in separate places and at the same time or at different times.

Because the term *copies* also refers to the original copy of the artwork, any time you lend, lease, give possession, or transfer the original copy or a reproduction, you may have published the work even if only a single copy is distributed. Thus, any time you do any of these things, you must put a notice on all publicly distributed copies.

The Copyright Act spells out exceptions to the rule. A mere public display does not constitute a publication; thus, merely hanging your work on a wall—even on a wall where a "substantial" number of people outside your family and friends will see it—doesn't amount to a publication. Also, under the doctrine of "limited publication," if you merely give out a few copies of your work for purposes of criticism, comment, or review, with the understanding that these copies will be returned after being reviewed, then this is not a true publication requiring the use of a copyright notice. Of course, my recommendation is to use the notice anyway, even when you think yours is only a limited publication.

What's Included in a Copyright Notice

The copyright notice does many things. For instance, it tells the public that someone is claiming a copyright in the work. It shows when the work was first published and thus gives information about how long the copyright will last. It also shows who the owner is, so people who want licenses will have someone to contact and so anyone wanting to check Copyright Office records for a registration can identify the registration by owner.

A proper notice includes the following three elements:

1. the copyright symbol ©, or alternatively the word *Copyright* or the abbreviation *Copr.*;
2. the year date of first publication (*not* the exact month-day-year date); and
3. the name of the copyright owner or an alternative designation under which the owner is known.

My recommendation is to always use the international copyright symbol in order to get international protection. Spelling out the word *Copyright* or using the abbreviation *Copr.* may get you U.S. protection but does not ensure extraterritorial protection. If you think people won't understand what the copyright symbol means, then use *Copyright* in addition to the international symbol. Preferably, the word should appear before the symbol.

The year date of first publication is the year you first publicly distributed copies. This date always remains with the notice even if you later revise the work. For example, if you first published the work in 1977 and published a revised version in 1986, a proper notice would be:

© 1977, 1986 [Your Name].

You may notice that some owners use roman numerals for the date; some case law even supports this usage in the United States. But roman numerals are often employed because many people can't read these numerals, and the copyright owner wants to obscure the true date of first publication in order to hide how old the work is. I don't recommend using them.

Sometimes dates don't have to be used. As the statute says:

> The year date may be omitted where a pictorial, graphic, or sculptural work, with accompanying text matter, if any, is reproduced in or on greeting cards, postcards, stationery, jewelry, dolls, toys, or any useful articles.

Unless you have good reason for omitting the date under this exception, don't do it.

If you are the copyright owner, then use your full name. You may also use your first and middle initials in addition to your surname. Sometimes if you're known merely by your surname, it alone will suffice. Do not use fictitious names *unless* you have complied with local and state laws concerning fictitious name statements. Typically, such laws require you to file and publish fictitious name statements in the localities where you do business under the fictitious name. The reason for filing before using the fictitious name in the notice is that the law requires you to use "a generally known alternative designation of the owner."

All elements of the notice must appear immediately together, preferably on one line. If you want, you can add the words "All Rights Reserved" below the notice to give you possible further protection under the Buenos Aires Convention.

Here are examples of proper notices:

- Preferred minimum copyright notice for single owner—satisfies Universal Copyright Convention:
  © 1987 John Doe
- Less preferred alternatives for minimum copyright notice for single owner:
  Copyright 1987 John Doe
  Copr. 1987 John Doe
- Minimum copyright notice for joint owners:
  © 1987 John Doe and Jane Roe
- Commonly used extra feature notice:
  Copyright © 1987 Jane Roe
- Notice for work published in more than one edition:
  © 1987, 1988, 1990 Jane Roe
- Notice incorporating Buenos Aires Convention words:
  © 1987 Jane Roe
  All Rights Reserved
- Notice for separate contributions to composite or collective work:
  © 1985 John Doe (photographs)
  © 1987 Jane Roe (text)

Placement of Notices

The law requires placement of the notice to give "reasonable notice of the claim of copyright." Just as a filmmaker can't place a subliminal notice on one frame of film in the middle of a film, and a writer can't place a notice in the middle of the text in a book, artists can't use microscopic notices or notices affixed in obscure places. Typically, you should place a sufficiently large notice on the front of the work if at all possible. If you're putting it on the margin, make sure that the margin will show up if the work is published or framed. You don't want notices covered up or cropped out. If you can't put it on the front, place it on the back, frame, pedestal, or some similar spot.

Defective Notices

What happens if the notice is erroneous? If you omit one of the three major elements, that's equivalent to using no notice at all. Failure to use the copyright symbol or its equivalent, or to give the date or the copyright owner's name, increases the chance that the work will fall into the public domain. (See page 25 for steps you can take to protect yourself.)

What happens if the date is there but it's wrong, or the name is there but it's wrong?

If you use a year that is earlier than the year of first publication, you have not made a serious mistake. The copyright is valid, but any term of protection or presumption as to the date of the author's death that is based upon the date of first publication will begin to run from the date in the notice and not from the true date of first publication. However, if the date is more than one year late, this is more serious. You should follow the remedies on page 26. The purpose here is to prevent owners from giving an impression that the term of protection extends for a longer period.

Using the wrong name is not always a serious error. For example, if the notice appears in the name of your publisher or other licensee, the copyright will remain valid. Nonetheless, you might have to pay a penalty. Anyone relying on such a notice may take a license from the person named in the notice and have a complete defense against you even if you did not consent to the license. The purpose is to compel the true owner to give public notice of his name. (This rule does not apply if the notice was affixed by someone having no right to publish your work.)

For example, if you give a corporation an exclusive license to distribute copies of your work, and your corporate licensee not only uses its own copyright notice but also improperly grants a sublicense to a third person to exploit the work, that third person may have a complete defense against you if he honestly relied upon the name in the notice. One way to prevent this problem is to have a written agreement requiring your licensee to put your name in the notice affixed to all licensed copies.

If the wrong name is used, you can remedy the situation by immediately registering the copyright in your name. The registration gives public notice of the true owner's name, so that no one can claim they relied merely upon the name in the notice.

One special case of someone else's name in the notice is the publisher's notice in a collective work. Frequently a magazine publisher will use its notice in the masthead without using notices for any contributing writers and artists. Generally the publisher's notice protects the entire collective work and all contributions in it, with one exception. If your artwork appears in an advertisement inserted on behalf of someone other than the copyright owner of the magazine, the publisher's notice will not suffice, and the advertisement must bear its own notice. For example, many fine artists allow gallery owners to publish advertisements that contain reproductions of the artists' works. Usually these advertisements appear without copyright notices, thus jeopardizing the artists' copyrights in the reproduced works.

Remedies for Errors

Take heart. Under the new copyright laws, failure to use a proper notice is not always fatal. Under the 1909 Copyright Act, if notice were omitted from more than a limited number of published copies, the work was usually injected into the public domain. However, you'll be relieved to know that under the Copyright Revision Act of 1976, the copyright is not invalidated if the notice has been omitted from no more than a relatively small number of copies distributed to the public. The key word here is *relatively*. Of a million published copies, perhaps one hundred copies without notice will not invalidate the copyright, but of only one thousand published copies, perhaps five hundred copies without notice will invalidate the copyright.

Also, the copyright is not lost if registration is made within five years after the publication without notice and a reasonable effort is made to add the notice to all copies distributed in the United States after the omission is discovered. The key term here is *reasonable effort*, which means that you must sometimes try to contact all people who have received copies without notices, and perhaps even send them stick-on labels bearing the copyright notice along with instructions to place the labels on the copies.

Finally, the copyright is not lost if the notice has been omitted in violation of an express requirement in writing that, as a condition of your permission to publicly distribute copies, they bear the prescribed notice. So whenever you license someone to reproduce and/or distribute copies of your work, you should have a written agreement specifying that the notice must be affixed to all copies.

Even though the new Copyright Act lets you keep your rights if you take certain remedial measures, the omission of a notice usually has some adverse effects. For example, any person who innocently infringes the copyright after relying on copies that you allowed to be published without the notice is not liable to you for actual or statutory damages or for any infringing acts committed before receiving notice that registration for the work has been made, if that person can prove that he was misled by the omission of the notice. In an infringement suit against such an innocent infringer, the court may award you profits or an injunction, but whether or not you are awarded anything is totally within the court's discretion.

REGISTRATION

Since a copyright exists from the moment the work is *fixed*, and since the copyright is maintained by using notices on published copies, why register copyrights? First, registration is a prerequisite to bringing a lawsuit. In other words, until your registration is actually granted, you generally can't sue anyone for copyright infringement.

Second, with copyright registration, the early bird gets the worm. If someone in-

fringes your copyright before you register it, you can't recover statutory damages and attorney's fees, extremely important remedies in any infringement case. The only exception to this rule is a three-month grace period. If you register within three months after first publishing the work and the infringement occurs after your first publication, then you can still get all the remedies.

Third, in any court proceeding, the certificate of a registration made before or within five years after first publication of the work constitutes *prima facie* evidence of the validity of the copyright and the facts stated in the certificate.

So my advice is to register as many works as possible. Naturally, this is not always economically feasible, so you have some choices to make. If you don't have the time and money to register all your works, then at least register those that are most likely to be copied, that have taken the longest to produce, are most valuable to you, and, if unlawfully copied, might result in huge profits for the infringer.

Procedure

Copyright registration requires four things:

1. the filled-in application form;
2. deposit copy(s) of the work;
3. a money order or check; and
4. a cover letter sent with the application.

All materials are sent to the U.S. Copyright Office, a branch of the Library of Congress. The address is: Register of Copyrights, Library of Congress, Washington, DC 20559. The fee for each work is currently ten dollars.

Filling Out Copyright Registration Forms

The Copyright Office has several different registration forms. The following describes the forms most likely encountered by a fine or graphic artist:

■ Form VA: For "works of visual arts," such as drawings, sculptures, paintings, and photographs. This is the form most commonly used by artists.

- Form TX: For "nondramatic literary works," such as books, brochures, monographs, and computer programs.
- Form PA: For "works of performing arts," such as plays, musical compositions, choreographic works, motion picture films, and other audiovisual works.
- Form SR: For "sound recordings."
- Form CA: For supplementing or correcting an earlier-filed registration certificate.
- Form GR/CP: For a group of works contributed to various periodicals but only as an adjunct form in connection with basic forms PA, VA, and TX.
- Form SE: For serials, such as magazines, newspapers, and other periodicals.
- Form RE: For renewing copyrights secured under the 1909 Act.

All forms come with instructions, and each has supplemental forms in case the registrant needs more room for all required information. For example, the supplementary form for Form VA is Form VA/CON, which is a continuation form for Form VA.

Form VA, shown on the following pages, is usually a simple form to fill out. However, this example is more complicated than usual in order to illustrate as many terms as possible. In this case, John H. Doe, an author/illustrator, worked in-house at the X-Ray Corporation as an independent contractor. In his contract, Doe agreed to transfer to the corporation all rights to the work named "Hope Springs Eternal" (Space 1). Doe and the corporation are both listed as authors in Space 2, since Doe is the anonymous author and the corporation is the copyright-holder. However, the corporation is the claimant (Space 4) since it owns the copyright. Since the work was previously published and registered (Spaces 3 and 5), it is considered a derivative piece (Space 6). Space 7 is not filled in, because the corporation does not have a Deposit Account in the Copyright Office and, instead, sent $10

with the application and deposit. Spaces 8 and 9 show that the corporation's agent, Jane Roe, completed the form. Notice that copyright forms, like tax forms, must be signed and dated.

I've also given you copies of the instructions for Form VA on pages 21-22. These are very complete instructions. You should look at these instructions carefully along with the sample filled-in form.

The following comments supplement the Form VA instructions provided by the Copyright Office. If the Copyright Office instructions are complete or complete enough to enable you to make intelligent choices in most situations, I will not comment.

Comments on Form VA

At Space 1 where you indicate the "nature of this work," be sure to put in an adequate description. You will be surprised how the works are actually described. For example, a doll may be a "soft sculpture."

At Space 2 where it asks for the "name of author," use a full expression of your name, and if you use a fictitious business name or alias or shortened version of your name in connection with the work, you may want to indicate the "DBA" or "AKA" alternative name under which you are known.

Also at Space 2, if you check the box to indicate that the contribution to the work was a "work made for hire," you are doing so to indicate that you, as the author, were the "employer for hire." In other words, you did not create the work but hired someone else to create it. If you originated the work for someone else as a work made for hire, you cannot file for copyright in your name.

In Space 2 where you indicate the nationality or domicile of the author, be aware that it helps if you or at least one other author is a citizen or domiciliary of the United States; such a status helps secure U.S. copyright protection.

At Space 2 where it asks for "nature of authorship," the request is for the type of artistic contribution made by the author, but perhaps not in the way you think. If two authors collaborate on putting out a photo book with text, one author might indicate "photographs" and the other author "text" or "entire text." But what happens if one author does a black-and-white ink illustration that a co-author colors in? It's tempting to say one author contributed the "ink illustration" while the other author did the "coloring." However, the correct answer, or at least a correct answer, for each author would be "co-author of illustration," since the artists' contributions can't readily be separated or isolated.

Remember that to be a contributor, an author does not have to pick up a pen, camera, brush, or chisel. For instance, for a book of illustrations with text, the artist may receive many suggestions from the writer, and vice versa. For both authors, the "nature of authorship" would read "co-author of entire work" or "co-author of text and illustrations."

At Space 3 where it asks for the year in which creation was completed, you put in that year in which creation was actually finished. When you register a later version of a work created years before, you use the year when the derivative work was finally completed.

The same applies to "date and nation of first publication of this particular work" at Space 3. If you are registering the copyright for a derivative work, you use the publication date for the derivative work, not for the original.

By the way, sometimes it's almost impossible, or actually impossible, to determine the exact date that publication first took place. If it is impossible but you can narrow the time period down to a week or two, you won't seriously jeopardize your application if you take your best guess.

If the copyright is being registered in the creators' names, make sure that the names appear identically at Space 2 and Space 4.

If the copyright is being registered in someone else's name, an indication of transfer should appear at Space 4.

At Space 5, if you have filed an earlier application for a prior edition or prior version of the work but registration has not been issued, where it asks for "previous registration number," put "registration pending."

Please be careful at Space 6 in defining the "material added to this work." It's this later material that will be protected by the copyright and *not* the pre-existing material. Also, remember what I said about the nature of authorship. If you have a black-and-white ink illustration and you add color, at Space 6(b) you do not say "added coloring." What you might say is "additional artistic work."

Deposit Copies

One thing not fully discussed in the instructions is what to do with the deposit copies. Moreover, the deposits are incompletely described.

For almost all artistic works, deposits consist of photographic depictions of the original work. Mostly, you send in either transparencies or prints of your work.

If you send in a transparency, it has to be no smaller than 35mm, and if smaller than 3x3, it must be mounted on cardboard or other suitable material. If you use prints, they must be no smaller than 3x3 and no larger than 9x12; the preferred size is 8x10. When taking the photographs, make sure the work doesn't take up the entire surface of the print or transparency so that you can see where the work ends and have space to indicate the measurements.

Use color transparencies and prints. Use black-and-white only if the work itself is in black and white.

Remember that whatever you send in establishes the scope of the registered copyright. The photographs must show your work as accurately as possible. For instance, if you created a three-dimensional work, you would want to send in enough photographs to show all aspects of the work, including front views, side views, perhaps bottom views, and views from other angles.

At least one piece of identifying material must have marked on it the title of the

(Continued on page 23)

FORM VA
UNITED STATES COPYRIGHT OFFICE

REGISTRATION NUMBER

VA   VAU

EFFECTIVE DATE OF REGISTRATION

Month   Day   Year

DO NOT WRITE ABOVE THIS LINE. IF YOU NEED MORE SPACE, USE A SEPARATE CONTINUATION SHEET.

1

TITLE OF THIS WORK ▼

Hope Springs Eternal

NATURE OF THIS WORK ▼ See instructions

ink drawing with text

PREVIOUS OR ALTERNATIVE TITLES ▼

PUBLICATION AS A CONTRIBUTION If this work was published as a contribution to a periodical, serial, or collection, give information about the collective work in which the contribution appeared. **Title of Collective Work ▼**

If published in a periodical or serial give: **Volume ▼**   **Number ▼**   **Issue Date ▼**   **On Pages ▼**

2

a

NAME OF AUTHOR ▼

John H. Doe dba Artsmart

DATES OF BIRTH AND DEATH
Year Born ▼ 1954   Year Died ▼

Was this contribution to the work a "work made for hire"?
☐ Yes
☒ No

AUTHOR'S NATIONALITY OR DOMICILE
Name of Country
OR { Citizen of ▶ U.S.A.
{ Domiciled in ▶

WAS THIS AUTHOR'S CONTRIBUTION TO THE WORK
Anonymous? ☒ Yes ☐ No
Pseudonymous? ☐ Yes ☒ No
If the answer to either of these questions is "Yes," see detailed instructions.

NATURE OF AUTHORSHIP Briefly describe nature of the material created by this author in which copyright is claimed. ▼

artwork, co-author of text

NOTE

Under the law, the "author" of a "work made for hire" is generally the employer, not the employee (see instructions). For any part of this work that was "made for hire" check "Yes" in the space provided, give the employer (or other person for whom the work was prepared) as "Author" of that part, and leave the space for dates of birth and death blank.

b

NAME OF AUTHOR ▼

X-Ray Corporation dba X-Ray Cards

DATES OF BIRTH AND DEATH
Year Born ▼   Year Died ▼

Was this contribution to the work a "work made for hire"?
☒ Yes
☐ No

AUTHOR'S NATIONALITY OR DOMICILE
Name of country
OR { Citizen of ▶
{ Domiciled in ▶ U.S.A.

WAS THIS AUTHOR'S CONTRIBUTION TO THE WORK
Anonymous? ☐ Yes ☒ No
Pseudonymous? ☐ Yes ☒ No
If the answer to either of these questions is "Yes," see detailed instructions.

NATURE OF AUTHORSHIP Briefly describe nature of the material created by this author in which copyright is claimed. ▼

co-author of text

c

NAME OF AUTHOR ▼

DATES OF BIRTH AND DEATH
Year Born ▼   Year Died ▼

Was this contribution to the work a "work made for hire"?
☐ Yes
☐ No

AUTHOR'S NATIONALITY OR DOMICILE
Name of Country
OR { Citizen of ▶
{ Domiciled in ▶

WAS THIS AUTHOR'S CONTRIBUTION TO THE WORK
Anonymous? ☐ Yes ☐ No
Pseudonymous? ☐ Yes ☐ No
If the answer to either of these questions is "Yes," see detailed instructions.

NATURE OF AUTHORSHIP Briefly describe nature of the material created by this author in which copyright is claimed. ▼

3

YEAR IN WHICH CREATION OF THIS WORK WAS COMPLETED This information must be given in all cases. 1987 ◀ Year

DATE AND NATION OF FIRST PUBLICATION OF THIS PARTICULAR WORK
Complete this information ONLY if this work has been published.
Month ▶ January Day ▶ 07 Year ▶ 1988
U.S.A. ◀ Nation

4

COPYRIGHT CLAIMANT(S) Name and address must be given even if the claimant is the same as the author given in space 2.▼

X-Ray Corporation dba X-Ray Cards
1000 Main Street, Suite 100
Anytown, PA 17075

See instructions before completing this space.

APPLICATION RECEIVED

ONE DEPOSIT RECEIVED

TWO DEPOSITS RECEIVED

REMITTANCE NUMBER AND DATE

DO NOT WRITE HERE OFFICE USE ONLY

TRANSFER If the claimant(s) named here in space 4 are different from the author(s) named in space 2, give a brief statement of how the claimant(s) obtained ownership of the copyright.▼

Author John Doe transferred all of his rights by contract to the Claimant

MORE ON BACK ▶ • Complete all applicable spaces (numbers 5-9) on the reverse side of this page.
• See detailed instructions. • Sign the form at line 8.

DO NOT WRITE HERE

Page 1 of _____ pages

DO NOT WRITE ABOVE THIS LINE. IF YOU NEED MORE SPACE, USE A SEPARATE CONTINUATION SHEET.

PREVIOUS REGISTRATION Has registration for this work, or for an earlier version of this work, already been made in the Copyright Office?

☒ Yes ☐ No If your answer is "Yes," why is another registration being sought? (Check appropriate box) ▼

☒ This is the first published edition of a work previously registered in unpublished form.

☐ This is the first application submitted by this author as copyright claimant.

☐ This is a changed version of the work, as shown by space 6 on this application.

If your answer is "Yes," give: **Previous Registration Number** ▼   **Year of Registration** ▼

VAu 100—100   1987

5

DERIVATIVE WORK OR COMPILATION Complete both space 6a & 6b for a derivative work; complete only 6b for a compilation.

a. Preexisting Material Identify any preexisting work or works that this work is based on or incorporates. ▼

charcoal illustration with text

b. Material Added to This Work Give a brief, general statement of the material that has been added to this work and in which copyright is claimed.▼

new and altered artwork, new and altered text

See instructions before completing this space.

6

DEPOSIT ACCOUNT If the registration fee is to be charged to a Deposit Account established in the Copyright Office, give name and number of Account.

Name ▼   **Account Number** ▼

7

CORRESPONDENCE Give name and address to which correspondence about this application should be sent. Name/Address/Apt/City/State/Zip ▼

Ms. Jane Roe
X-Ray Corporation
1000 Main St., Ste. 100
Anytown, PA 17075

Area Code & Telephone Number ▶ (215) 555-1000

Be sure to give your daytime phone number ◀

8

CERTIFICATION* I, the undersigned, hereby certify that I am the

Check only one ▼

☐ author

☐ other copyright claimant

☐ owner of exclusive right(s)

☒ authorized agent of X-Ray Corporation
                        Name of author or other copyright claimant, or owner of exclusive right(s) ▲

of the work identified in this application and that the statements made
by me in this application are correct to the best of my knowledge.

Typed or printed name and date ▼ If this is a published work, this date must be the same as or later than the date of publication given in space 3.

JANE ROE   date ▶ 02/18/88

Handwritten signature (X) ▼

Jane Roe

9

MAIL CERTIFICATE TO

Name ▼
X-Ray Corporation

Number/Street/Apartment Number ▼
1000 Main St., Ste. 100

City/State/ZIP ▼
Anytown, PA 17075

Certificate will be mailed in window envelope

Have you:
• Completed all necessary spaces?
• Signed your application in space 8?
• Enclosed check or money order for $10 payable to *Register of Copyrights?*
• Enclosed your deposit material with the application and fee?

MAIL TO: Register of Copyrights, Library of Congress, Washington, D.C. 20559.

Filling Out Application Form VA

Detach and read these instructions before completing this form. Make sure all applicable spaces have been filled in before you return this form.

BASIC INFORMATION

When to Use This Form: Use Form VA for copyright registration of published or unpublished works of the visual arts. This category consists of "pictorial, graphic, or sculptural works," including two-dimensional and three-dimensional works of fine, graphic, and applied art, photographs, prints and art reproductions, maps, globes, charts, technical drawings, diagrams, and models.

What Does Copyright Protect? Copyright in a work of the visual arts protects those pictorial, graphic, or sculptural elements that, either alone or in combination, represent an "original work of authorship." The statute declares: "In no case does copyright protection for an original work of authorship extend to any idea, procedure, process, system, method of operation, concept, principle, or discovery, regardless of the form in which it is described, explained, illustrated, or embodied in such work."

Works of Artistic Craftsmanship and Designs: "Works of artistic craftsmanship" are registrable on Form VA, but the statute makes clear that protection extends to "their form" and not to "their mechanical or utilitarian aspects." The "design of a useful article" is considered copyrightable "only if, and only to the extent that, such design incorporates pictorial, graphic, or sculptural features that can be identified separately from, and are capable of existing independently of, the utilitarian aspects of the article."

Labels and Advertisements: Works prepared for use in connection with the sale or advertisement of goods and services are registrable if they contain "original work of authorship." Use Form VA if the copyrightable material in the work you are registering is mainly pictorial or graphic; use Form TX if it consists mainly of text. **NOTE:** Words and short phrases such as names, titles, and slogans cannot be protected by copyright, and the same is true of standard symbols, emblems, and other commonly used graphic designs that are in the public domain. When used commercially, material of that sort can sometimes be protected under state laws of unfair competition or under the Federal trademark laws. For information about trademark registration, write to the Commissioner of Patents and Trademarks, Washington, D.C. 20231.

Deposit to Accompany Application: An application for copyright registration must be accompanied by a deposit consisting of copies representing the entire work for which registration is to be made.

Unpublished Work: Deposit one complete copy.

Published Work: Deposit two complete copies of the best edition.

Work First Published Outside the United States: Deposit one complete copy of the first foreign edition.

Contribution to a Collective Work: Deposit one complete copy of the best edition of the collective work.

The Copyright Notice: For published works, the law provides that a copyright notice in a specified form "shall be placed on all publicly distributed copies from which the work can be visually perceived." Use of the copyright notice is the responsibility of the copyright owner and does not require advance permission from the Copyright Office. The required form of the notice for copies generally consists of three elements: (1) the symbol "©", or the word "Copyright," or the abbreviation "Copr."; (2) the year of first publication; and (3) the name of the owner of copyright. For example: "© 1981 Constance Porter." The notice is to be affixed to the copies "in such manner and location as to give reasonable notice of the claim of copyright."

For further information about copyright registration, notice, or special questions relating to copyright problems, write:

Information and Publications Section, LM-455
Copyright Office, Library of Congress, Washington, D.C. 20559

LINE-BY-LINE INSTRUCTIONS

1 SPACE 1: Title

Title of This Work: Every work submitted for copyright registration must be given a title to identify that particular work. If the copies of the work bear a title (or an identifying phrase that could serve as a title), transcribe that wording *completely* and *exactly* on the application. Indexing of the registration and future identification of the work will depend on the information you give here.

Previous or Alternative Titles: Complete this space if there are any additional titles for the work under which someone searching for the registration might be likely to look, or under which a document pertaining to the work might be recorded.

Publication as a Contribution: If the work being registered is a contribution to a periodical, serial, or collection, give the title of the contribution in the "Title of This Work" space. Then, in the line headed "Publication as a Contribution," give information about the collective work in which the contribution appeared.

Nature of This Work: Briefly describe the general nature or character of the pictorial, graphic, or sculptural work being registered for copyright. Examples: "Oil Painting"; "Charcoal Drawing"; "Etching"; "Sculpture"; "Map"; "Photograph"; "Scale Model"; "Lithographic Print"; "Jewelry Design"; "Fabric Design."

2 SPACE 2: Author(s)

General Instructions: After reading these instructions, decide who are the "authors" of this work for copyright purposes. Then, unless the work is a "collective work," give the requested information about every "author" who contributed any appreciable amount of copyrightable matter to this version of the work. If you need further space, request additional Continuation Sheets. In the case of a collective work, such as a catalog of paintings or collection of cartoons by various authors, give information about the author of the collective work as a whole.

Name of Author: The fullest form of the author's name should be given. Unless the work was "made for hire," the individual who actually created the work is its "author." In the case of a work made for hire, the statute provides that "the employer or other person for whom the work was prepared is considered the author."

What is a "Work Made for Hire"? A "work made for hire" is defined as: (1) "a work prepared by an employee within the scope of his or her employment"; or (2) "a work specially ordered or commissioned for use as a contribution to a collective work, as a part of a motion picture or other audiovisual work, as a translation, as a supplementary work, as a compilation, as an instructional text, as a test, as answer material for a test, or as an atlas, if the parties expressly agree in a written instrument signed by them that the work shall be considered a work made for hire." If you have checked "Yes" to indicate that the work was "made for hire," you must give the full legal name of the employer (or other person for whom the work was prepared). You may also include the name of the employee along with the name of the employer (for example: "Elster Publishing Co., employer for hire of John Ferguson").

"Anonymous" or "Pseudonymous" Work: An author's contribution to a work is "anonymous" if that author is not identified on the copies or phonorecords of the work. An author's contribution to a work is "pseudonymous" if that author is identified on the copies or phonorecords under a fictitious name. If the work is "anonymous" you may: (1) leave the line blank; or (2) state "anonymous" on the line; or (3) reveal the author's identity. If the work is "pseudonymous" you may: (1) leave the line blank; or (2) give the pseudonym and identify it as such (for example: "Huntley Haverstock, pseudonym"); or (3) reveal the author's name, making clear which is the real name and which is the pseudonym (for example: "Henry Leek, whose pseudonym is Priam Farrel"). However, the citizenship or domicile of the author **must** be given in all cases.

Dates of Birth and Death: If the author is dead, the statute requires that the year of death be included in the application unless the work is anonymous or pseudonymous. The author's birth date is optional, but is useful as a form of identification. Leave this space blank if the author's contribution was a "work made for hire."

Author's Nationality or Domicile: Give the country of which the author is a citizen, or the country in which the author is domiciled. Nationality or domicile **must** be given in all cases.

Nature of Authorship: Give a brief general statement of the nature of this particular author's contribution to the work. Examples: "Painting"; "Photograph"; "Silk Screen Reproduction"; "Co-author of Cartographic Material"; "Technical Drawing"; "Text and Artwork."

3 SPACE 3: Creation and Publication

General Instructions: Do not confuse "creation" with "publication." Every application for copyright registration must state "the year in which creation of the work was completed." Give the date and nation of first publication only if the work has been published.

Creation: Under the statute, a work is "created" when it is fixed in a copy or phonorecord for the first time. Where a work has been prepared over a period of time, the part of the work existing in fixed form on a particular date constitutes the created work on that date. The date you give here should be the year in which the author completed the particular version for which registration is now being sought, even if other versions exist or if further changes or additions are planned.

Publication: The statute defines "publication" as "the distribution of copies or phonorecords of a work to the public by sale or other transfer of ownership, or by rental, lease, or lending"; a work is also "published" if there has been an "offering to distribute copies or phonorecords to a group of persons for purposes of further distribution, public performance, or public display." Give the full date (month, day, year) when, and the country where, publication first occurred. If first publication took place simultaneously in the United States and other countries, it is sufficient to state "U.S.A."

4 SPACE 4: Claimant(s)

Name(s) and Address(es) of Copyright Claimant(s): Give the name(s) and address(es) of the copyright claimant(s) in this work even if the claimant is the same as the author. Copyright in a work belongs initially to the author of the work (including, in the case of a work made for hire, the employer or other person for whom the work was prepared). The copyright claimant is either the author of the work or a person or organization to whom the copyright initially belonging to the author has been transferred.

Transfer: The statute provides that, if the copyright claimant is not the author, the application for registration must contain "a brief statement of how the claimant obtained ownership of the copyright." If any copyright claimant named in space 4 is not an author named in space 2, give a brief, general statement summarizing the means by which that claimant obtained ownership of the copyright. Examples: "By written contract"; "Transfer of all rights by author"; "Assignment"; "By will." Do not attach transfer documents or other attachments or riders.

5 SPACE 5: Previous Registration

General Instructions: The questions in space 5 are intended to find out whether an earlier registration has been made for this work and, if so, whether there is any basis for a new registration. As a rule, only one basic copyright registration can be made for the same version of a particular work.

Same Version: If this version is substantially the same as the work covered by a previous registration, a second registration is not generally possible unless: (1) the work has been registered in unpublished form and a second registration is now being sought to cover this first published edition; or (2) some-

one other than the author is identified as copyright claimant in the earlier registration, and the author is now seeking registration in his or her own name. If either of these two exceptions apply, check the appropriate box and give the earlier registration number and date. Otherwise, do not submit Form VA; instead, write the Copyright Office for information about supplementary registration or recordation of transfers of copyright ownership.

Changed Version: If the work has been changed, and you are now seeking registration to cover the additions or revisions, check the last box in space 5, give the earlier registration number and date, and complete both parts of space 6 in accordance with the instructions below.

Previous Registration Number and Date: If more than one previous registration has been made for the work, give the number and date of the latest registration.

6 SPACE 6: Derivative Work or Compilation

General Instructions: Complete space 6 if this work is a "changed version," "compilation," or "derivative work," and if it incorporates one or more earlier works that have already been published or registered for copyright, or that have fallen into the public domain. A "compilation" is defined as "a work formed by the collection and assembling of preexisting materials or of data that are selected, coordinated, or arranged in such a way that the resulting work as a whole constitutes an original work of authorship." A "derivative work" is "a work based on one or more preexisting works." Examples of derivative works include reproductions of works of art, sculptures based on drawings, lithographs based on paintings, maps based on previously published sources, or "any other form in which a work may be recast, transformed, or adapted." Derivative works also include works "consisting of editorial revisions, annotations, or other modifications" if these changes, as a whole, represent an original work of authorship.

Preexisting Material (space 6a): Complete this space **and** space 6b for derivative works. In this space identify the preexisting work that has been recast, transformed, or adapted. Examples of preexisting material might be "Grunewald Altarpiece"; or "19th century quilt design." Do not complete this space for compilations.

Material Added to This Work (space 6b): Give a brief, general statement of the **additional** new material covered by the copyright claim for which registration is sought. In the case of a derivative work, identify this new material. Examples: "Adaptation of design and additional artistic work"; "Reproduction of painting by photolithography"; "Additional cartographic material"; "Compilation of photographs." If the work is a compilation, give a brief, general statement describing both the material that has been compiled **and** the compilation itself. Example: "Compilation of 19th Century Political Cartoons."

7,8,9 SPACE 7, 8, 9: Fee, Correspondence, Certification, Return Address

Deposit Account: If you maintain a Deposit Account in the Copyright Office, identify it in space 7. Otherwise leave the space blank and send the fee of $10 with your application and deposit.

Correspondence (space 7): This space should contain the name, address, area code, and telephone number of the person to be consulted if correspondence about this application becomes necessary.

Certification (space 8): The application cannot be accepted unless it bears the date and the **handwritten signature** of the author or other copyright claimant, or of the owner of exclusive right(s), or of the duly authorized agent of the author, claimant, or owner of exclusive right(s).

Address for Return of Certificate (space 9): The address box must be completed legibly since the certificate will be returned in a window envelope.

MORE INFORMATION

Form of Deposit for Works of the Visual Arts

Exceptions to General Deposit Requirements: As explained on the reverse side of this page, the statutory deposit requirements (generally one copy for unpublished works and two copies for published works) will vary for particular kinds of works of the visual arts. The copyright law authorizes the Register of Copyrights to issue regulations specifying "the administrative classes into which works are to be placed for purposes of deposit and registration, and the nature of the copies or phonorecords to be deposited in the various classes specified." For particular classes, the regulations may require or permit "the deposit of identifying material instead of copies or phonorecords," or "the deposit of only one copy or phonorecord where two would normally be required."

What Should You Deposit? The detailed requirements with respect to the kind of deposit to accompany an application on Form VA are contained in the Copyright

Office Regulations. The following does not cover all of the deposit requirements, but is intended to give you some general guidance.

For an Unpublished Work, the material deposited should represent the entire copyrightable content of the work for which registration is being sought.

For a Published Work, the material deposited should generally consist of two complete copies of the best edition. Exceptions: (1) For certain types of works, one complete copy may be deposited instead of two. These include greeting cards, postcards, stationery, labels, advertisements, scientific drawings, and globes; (2) For most three-dimensional sculptural works, and for certain two-dimensional works, the Copyright Office Regulations require deposit of identifying material (photographs or drawings in a specified form) rather than copies; and (3) Under certain circumstances, for works published in five copies or less or in limited, numbered editions, the deposit may consist of one copy or of identifying reproductions.

work and at least one dimension in inches. I encourage you to put the following information on the identifying material: the name(s) of the claimant(s); the title of the work; and two dimensions, such as height and width of the original work.

If the dimension being measured is not apparent from the photograph, you should indicate at least one dimension with lines and arrows along with the corresponding measurement.

With published works, at least one piece of identifying material should show the use of the notice on the copies. If the photographic views of the work do not depict the notice, you may have to use a close-up shot. If a close-up shot doesn't work, the Copyright Office requires a drawing depicting the content of the copyright notice and its location on the work.

Revising the Application

Sometimes the application will be sent back to you, especially if you failed to submit one of the necessary components, such as the check. Other times it won't be sent back, but you will get a letter from a Copyright Office examiner asking you to correct the application. The examiner usually explains what is wrong and makes suggestions for correction. You must promptly reply to the examiner by letter, enclosing a copy of the examiner's letter to you, and take some action to correct the application, or your application will be deemed abandoned.

Don't worry about the examiner's response moving back the effective date of registration. The date of registration is the date on which the application, deposit, and fee, acceptable for registration, have all been received by the Copyright Office. So if your application is basically complete, and the examiner has only minor corrections, the date of receipt will be used as the date of registration. Even though the certificate of registration may issue months later, the registration is back-dated to that original date. If you are worried about having your materials arrive at the Copyright Office, send them by registered mail or by reputa-

ble overnight mail carriers offering return-receipt services.

It is usually best to adopt the examiner's suggestions for changes if your application is initially rejected or otherwise sent back to you. On the other hand, please remember that examiners can be wrong, especially in denying registration to certain works because they are not copyrightable. If you doubt an examiner's determination, consult an attorney.

Any time you need help with registration, you can call the Copyright Office information number (202)479-0700. You can also write for information, forms, and Copyright Office circulars to: Information and Publications, Section LM-455, Copyright Office, Library of Congress, Washington, DC 20559.

When to Seek Legal Help

Please remember that the registration form can be deceptively simple. The determination of who is the author, whether the work is "made for hire," the date of first publication, and other matters sometimes requires legal knowledge you don't have. In addition, if there are other authors besides you and you want to register as the sole claimant, you will need transfer documents or work-made-for-hire agreements that may require an attorney's help.

I suggest that, if you have never done an application, then let an attorney do the first one for you. This can be a good learning process, and you may then be able to do the rest of the applications yourself with only a little help from an attorney.

It's a good idea to use an attorney to register any work that is very important for you. You don't want to get a registration certificate back from the Copyright Office that isn't worth the paper it's printed on.

PUBLIC ACCESS TO COPYRIGHT OFFICE RECORDS

The Register of Copyrights makes records of all deposits, registrations, recordings, and other actions taken by the Copyright Office and prepares indexes for these records. For example, there are indexes that show registrations by the names of the claimants and by the names of the works. These records are open to public inspection or, for people who can't inspect the records themselves, the Copyright Office will, for a small fee (currently ten dollars per hour plus costs), search its own records and furnish a report.

The Copyright Office also makes copies of its records, including registration certificates, and furnishes them to the public for a small fee.

The Copyright Office usually will *not* give out copies of works deposited along with registration applications, but you can inspect most deposits. Copying of deposits is allowed at the request of the copyright owner, by court order, or at the request of an attorney who needs a copy for litigation involving the copyrighted work.

Information Services and Forms

The Copyright Office publishes informational brochures called *circulars* that give information about what works are copyrightable, how to secure registrations, and most other matters covered by the Copyright Act. You can get these circulars and a list of circulars from the Copyright Office free of charge. Use the address on page 16.

The Copyright Office also will provide a free copy of Title 17, United States Code, the copyright legislation.

For general information concerning copyright, you may call during working hours, Eastern Standard Time, (202)479-0700. To request copyright forms, call (202)287-9100. You dial this number and leave a message giving your name and address, and how many and which forms you want.

DURATION OF COPYRIGHT

Copyrights can last for a long time, long enough to satisfy almost everyone. The general term extends from the creation of the work until fifty years after the author's death. For a joint work, the copyright extends fifty years beyond the death of the last surviving author.

With anonymous works, pseudonymous works, and works made for hire, the copyright endures for a term of seventy-five years from the year of first publication, or for one hundred years from creation, whichever expires first. For this purpose, an *anonymous work* is one where no natural person is identified as author, and a *pseudonymous work* is one where the author is identified under a fictitious name. (Obviously, if you want "life plus fifty years," then use your real name.)

See page 24 for more information on duration.

INFRINGEMENT

Infringement occurs when someone exercises one of your exclusive rights without consent. For example, if someone reproduces your work without authorization, he commits copyright infringement; the same is true if another person creates a sculpture based on your drawing. Anyone who distributes or publicly displays copies of your work without your consent is also an infringer, except persons who actually own the copies they publicly distribute or display.

It's easy to see that infringement has taken place when someone has reproduced your work exactly, or publicly distributed or displayed exact copies. But it's not necessarily so easy when the person has adapted the work or used only a small portion of it. Then a judge or jury has to determine whether copying actually took place.

Proving Infringement

You can prove infringement in one of two ways, through *direct evidence* or *circumstantial evidence*. Examples of direct evidence are admissions by the defendant that she copied or eyewitness testimony to the copying. Circumstantial evidence, on the other hand, is principally based on the similarity of the two works and the infringer's access to your work.

In proving a case circumstantially, the more access you can prove, the stronger the case; obviously, the more "substantial" similarity, the stronger the case. For instance, if the only copy of your work were locked up in a drawer to which the defendant had no access, it would be virtually impossible to prove copyright infringement. The opposite would be true if millions of copies were pub-

DURATION OF COPYRIGHT: PUBLIC DOMAIN WORKS

The following works are almost always in the public domain and may be copied after you consult an attorney:

- Works published before January 1, 1978 (the effective date of the 1976 Copyright Act), for which no renewal application was filed and registered with the Copyright Office during the twenty-eighth year of the first term of protection under the 1909 Copyright Act.
- Works created on or after January 1, 1978, for which the last surviving author has been dead for fifty years.
- Anonymous works, pseudonymous works, and works made for hire created on or after January 1, 1978, for which one hundred years has expired from the date of creation or seventy-five years has expired from the date of first publication.
- Works first published before January 1, 1978, for which renewal applications have been filed and registered under the 1909 Act and for which seventy-five years have expired from the date of first publication.
- All works created before January 1, 1978, not otherwise in the public domain nor published, have their copyrights expire no earlier than December 31, 2002, and, if published on or before December 31, 2002, have their copyrights expire no sooner than December 31, 2027.

Caution

Before copying someone else's work because you think it has slipped into the public domain, always consult an attorney. Many times the copy you looked at was published without consent of the copyright owner, so even though you believe the work was published on a certain date or without a copyright notice, you may be wrong. Sometimes you must search Copyright Office records, and only a qualified attorney can weigh the legal effects of various documents.

licly circulated. If the two works had a totally dissimilar appearance, infringement would be difficult to prove circumstantially, but if very similar, the case would be easier.

The easier it is to prove access, the less similarity you have to show, and vice versa. For example, if the works are virtually identical, you may not have to show very much access; also, if the public generally had access to your work because of widespread distribution, the similarity could be less.

In judging similarity, the judge or jury looks at not only the overall appearances of the two works but also minor details. In judging overall similarity, a judge or jury will look at the subject matter, form, and content of the respective works and even judge whether the aesthetic appeal is basically the same. In examining minor details, the court will look for common peculiarities. One common protection against infringement is to insert minor but harmless errors in the work; when an artist uses this technique, the infringer usually copies the errors and is caught red-handed. In a case involving a cartographer client, we caught an infringer because my mapmaker used an imaginary road that was copied onto another map.

Remember, to prove infringement, you don't have to show that the entire work was copied. If only 25 percent of your work were copied onto another work, or perhaps even only 10 percent, there may still be infringement. Thus, all the rumors about changing works 10 percent or 20 percent to avoid liability are completely false. However, with less copying, the award of damages may be less.

Independent Creation

Just because someone else's work looks like yours doesn't mean you can prove infringement. When someone has independently created a very similar work without copying, infringement has not taken place. Of course, the more widespread access you can prove, the more difficult for the defendant to prove independent creation. Moreover, if the content of your work can be obtained from many sources, it will more difficult to prove infringement. Whenever the defendant can prove she copied from an independent source, there is no infringement. For example, if you draw something that is very common subject matter, such as the Mona Lisa, you can't stop other people from drawing the very same subject matter, especially if they are going to the original source.

Strict Liability

Remember that you need not show that the defendant knew or should have known that he was infringing your copyright. This means that virtually anyone involved in reproducing or distributing copies of your work is liable. For instance, if the principal defendant reproduced your work in a book, all bookstore owners selling the book are committing copyright infringement; similarly, all printers who printed the book are guilty regardless of their knowledge.

If you sue these relatively innocent defendants, especially to recover their profits, you might ask, what happens to them? What they do is claim contribution and indemnification from the principal defendant who originally caused the infringement. In other words, they ask the principal defendant to pay them back for all losses they suffer from your claims.

REMEDIES

The remedies for copyright infringement include:

1. injunctions;
2. impoundment and other disposition of infringing articles;
3. awards of damages and profits;
4. awards of costs and attorney's fees; and
5. criminal penalties.

Let's review each of the remedies briefly.

Injunctions

If the court grants an injunction, then the defendant will be ordered to stop the infringing activities. This means the defendant will have to stop reproducing, adapting, or displaying the work or distributing copies. A defendant who doesn't obey the court's order can be held in contempt of court and fined or even imprisoned. However, an injunction binds only those defendants who are parties to the action and only those parties served with the injunction papers.

There are three types of injunctive relief: First, you can procure a *temporary restraining order* by filing your complaint with the court along with supporting papers showing that emergency relief is needed. The temporary restraining order will prevent further infringement pending a hearing on a preliminary injunction.

A *preliminary injunction* is issued, usually early in the case, if the plaintiff can demonstrate that he or she is very likely to win the case. Such a preliminary injunction will be in effect during the pendency of the copyright action. Usually the court will issue a preliminary injunction only if you, the plaintiff, post a bond. The bond acts as security for the defendant, because if the defendant wins the lawsuit, the bond is used to compensate him for any injury incurred as a result of the preliminary injunction.

A *permanent injunction* is one that issues after the court renders a judgment for the plaintiff. This is the ultimate remedy, since it permanently stops infringement of the copyright.

Impoundment

Impoundment of infringing articles is also a very effective remedy. The court can seize all plates, molds, matrices, masters, tapes, film negatives, and other articles used to reproduce your work. Moreover, as part of a final judgment, the court may order the destruction or other reasonable disposition of all infringing copies and all articles used to reproduce your work.

Damages

In most lawsuits, the plaintiff is primarily concerned with awards of damages and profits.

Actual damages are awarded to compensate the copyright owner for losses. For example, if the plaintiff has lost sales because of the infringement, an award of actual damages may be equivalent to the profits the plaintiff would have made. If the infringing activities have totally destroyed the value of the copyright, the court can measure and award that value. Sometimes when the infringing activities have reduced or destroyed the value of the plaintiff's copyright, a court may even award an amount to compensate the owner for the time, effort, and expense of creating the copyrighted work.

Profits

In addition, the plaintiff may be entitled to an award of the defendant's profits. However, by *profits*, we mean *net profits*. Typically, the plaintiff must prove the defendant's gross revenues, and the defendant then proves his deductible expenses and the elements of profit attributable to factors other than the copyrighted work. This means that once you establish a defendant's revenues, he can deduct costs of manufacture, distribution, and labor, and sometimes even an allocable proportion of overhead. Furthermore, to reduce net profits even further, the defendant is entitled to an *apportionment*. For instance, if the infringing work is one-tenth your work and nine-tenths the infringer's own contributions, you will be entitled to only one-tenth of the net profits.

Please note that there is no double recovery of profits and damages. A plaintiff can recover only those profits of the defendant attributable to the infringement and not already taken into account in computing the actual damages. For instance, if you lost $10,000 in sales because of the infringement, and the defendant made $10,000 by selling to the very same customers whose sales you lost, you can choose either the profits or the damages, but you can't recover $20,000.

Statutory Damages

If you are a *prior registrant*, in other words, if you registered before the infringement or within the three-month grace period, you may elect any time before final judgment to recover *statutory damages* in lieu of actual damages and profits.

Statutory damages are awarded at the discretion of the court—within prescribed limits. The general limits are a minimum of $250, which the court must award, and a maximum of $10,000 per infringement. The bottom limit can be reduced to as little as $100 if the court finds that the infringement was innocent, and may be increased to $50,000 if the court finds that the infringement was committed willfully. If the infringer is a nonprofit educational institution, library, archives, public broadcasting entity, or an agent or employee thereof, who believed and had reasonable grounds for believing that the use of the copyrighted work was a *fair use*, the plaintiff may receive no statutory damages.

The court's discretion is almost absolute, but generally speaking, statutory damages should be comparable to the actual damages and profits. If the actual damages and profits were approximately $5,000, statutory damages will usually be approximately the same. However, this need not be so. If the court finds that infringement was willful, it can punish the defendant and award the full $50,000, even if profits and actual damages were much less.

Please remember that the statutory amounts are awarded *per infringement*. If your lawsuit is based on three separate copyrights, the court can give you three separate statutory awards. However, if three separate infringements of one copyright have been committed and you sue on all three infringements in one court action, the court may not be able to give three separate awards against one defendant.

Attorney's Fees

The losing party may be required to pay the other side's attorney's fees. Generally speaking, if infringement is proved, attorney's fees will be awarded only if the infringement and the defendant's defense of the case are characterized by some element of moral blame. A defendant who has a plausible, fair use defense or any other bona fide defense can usually avoid an award of attorney's fees.

Similarly, if no infringement is proved, attorney's fees will be awarded only if the plaintiff has brought a frivolous action. A plaintiff who loses on a technicality will usually not face such an award.

Criminal Proceedings

Filing a criminal complaint usually doesn't result in prosecution. You may legitimately complain only if you can show that the defendant willfully infringed for commercial gain. Most U.S. attorneys will not commence criminal proceedings, simply because they prefer to see copyright cases decided among the parties concerned.

Please note that criminal proceedings involve not only criminal copyright infringement but also fraudulent use and fraudulent removal of copyright notices. Anyone who places a false notice on your work or who fraudulently removes or alters your notice can be prosecuted.

DEFENSES

If you're taken to court for copyright infringement—or if you're suing someone else for infringement of your copyright—several different defenses may be used.

Innocent Intent

Innocent intent is usually not a complete defense. Even if you think you haven't infringed a copyright, an attorney confirms your opinion, or you copy a work pirated by someone else who omitted the true owner's copyright notice, you'll still be guilty of infringement.

Nonetheless, if the defendant can show that he did not intend to infringe, the award may be reduced. For example, where the defendant innocently infringed because the plaintiff didn't use a copyright notice on published copies of the work, the award may be limited to profits or to a reasonable license fee set by the court. Also, where the

defendant proves he was not aware and had no reason to believe that his acts constituted copyright infringement, an award of statutory damages can be as little as $100. Obviously, the defendant who shows innocent intent won't be criminally prosecuted, since criminal prosecution requires willful infringement for commercial gain; neither will the defendant be subject to paying $50,000 in statutory damages, since an award of that amount also requires willful infringement.

Fair Use

The *fair use* defense allows copyrighted material to be used for purposes such as criticism, comment, news reporting, teaching (including multiple copies for classroom use), scholarship, and research.

One purpose is to permit socially productive uses of the copyrighted work. These uses usually don't destroy the value of the copyright, even though they constitute technical infringements.

The factors that determine whether the use is "fair" include:

■ *The purpose and character of the use, including whether such use is of a commercial nature or is for nonprofit educational purposes.* The more commercial the use, the weaker the defense. Clearly, criticism, comment, news reporting, and other uses previously mentioned are the best qualifying uses, even if they are commercial uses.

■ *The nature of the copyrighted work.* Many factors about the work itself influence fair use. For instance, a published work that is out of print may be more susceptible to fair use because the defendant may have had more justification for copying than if the work were freely available. Compilations and databases are more susceptible than creative works, perhaps because creative works receive more sympathetic treatment in most areas of copyright law. Also, defendants who copy works targeted for special audiences and market the copies to the same audience will have more difficulty claiming fair use. For instance, the defendant who copies news items and artwork out of a specialty newsletter and out of a general circulation newspaper may have a fair use defense for copying the newspaper but not for copying the newsletter.

■ *The amount and substantiality of the portion used in relation to the copyrighted work as a whole.* In other words, the more of the work you use, the weaker the defense. This factor applies especially to cases involving parody. If you want the fair use defense when parodying another's work, you must use the minimum amount of the original work needed to give the impression of that work.

■ *The effect of the use on the potential market for or value of the copyrighted work.* In my mind, this is the most important factor. It's not easy to find a fair use if the defendant directly competes with the plaintiff, or if the defendant's use destroys the market for the original work. Clearly, criticism, comment, and news reporting usually do not involve competitive uses and usually, with the possible exception of criticism, do not destroy the market for the copyrighted work.

The above four factors are not exclusive. Another important factor, for example, is credits. If you want to use someone else's work and have a fair use defense, then put the creator's copyright notice and credits on those portions of the work you have copied (if doing so doesn't harm the creator's reputation by presenting her credits out of context). This way you won't be engaged in plagiarism, and you protect the author's interests as the original creator and copyright owner.

If you use original copyrighted works in classroom teaching, especially if you use multiple copies, some criteria for fair use are *brevity, spontaneity,* and *credit.* For example, the shorter the excerpt used, the better. The spontaneous use is more likely a fair use, so a teacher who copies the same materials year after year will usually not have the defense, whereas a one-shot, spontaneous use is more likely an eligible use.

The teacher should always use the copyright notice appearing on the original work, or at least a credit for the original author, even if the original work did not have a copyright notice.

What is a fair use is rarely clear-cut, and each case stands on its own merits. If you have any questions, ask a qualified attorney.

Delays in Enforcing

If the copyright owner knows about an infringement but doesn't enforce a copyright for a long time, a court may bar relief. However, the defendant must show that the delay is inexcusable and prejudicial to the defendant. Therefore, the innocent infringer has the best defense if he can show that time, effort, and money were invested in the infringing activities during the period of the plaintiff's inaction.

The defense is based on the notion that it is unfair for the copyright owner to remain inactive while the infringer spends large sums of money exploiting the infringing work, allowing the owner to intervene only when the infringer has made a success of it.

With this in mind, it's best to make a decision about suing within a few months, and sometimes even within a few weeks, after discovering the infringement. If you let a year, and sometimes even a lesser period, elapse, you may be unable to enforce your rights, even though the statute of limitations has not run on your claim.

Abandoned Copyrights

Where the copyright owner intends to give up his rights in the work, the copyright is deemed *abandoned*, and the defendant has a complete defense. Abandonment may occur, for example, where the owner deliberately publishes the work without a copyright notice or repeatedly fails to enforce the copyright in the face of blatant infringements.

Somewhat related to abandonment is the defense of *estoppel*. If the copyright owner knows about the infringement and gives the impression that the infringing activities will be tolerated when, in fact, the owner has no such intention, then the owner may be stopped from pursuing her claim. If the plaintiff helps the defendant with the defendant's infringing activities or directly or indirectly encourages the activities, there will be an estoppel even if the plaintiff secretly doesn't intend to permit the infringement. Many times a publisher or another artist will tell you that they don't mind your using their work even though they won't give you a license. In this situation, you may be able to use the estoppel defense if they change their mind after you begin your use.

Permission
If the defendant can show that the plaintiff consented to the defendant's use, this will be a complete defense. Thus, a valid licensing agreement provides a defense. Frequently a defendant relies on permission from the plaintiff's agent which the plaintiff may not know about, and such permission may furnish a defense.

Sometimes the permission or license is only implied. Be careful about implied permission, though. In one recent case I had, an artist who created designs for stained-glass works published a book of stained-glass design patterns. The book was published with an implicit understanding that anyone could copy the designs for personal use at home. However, when a large stained glass manufacturer copied the designs, the artist claimed that the permission did not extend to large-scale commercial use. The artist settled the case for a substantial amount.

Other Defenses
A rare defense called *unclean hands* is used when the plaintiff has engaged in unconscionable behavior relating to the subject matter of the lawsuit—for example, if the plaintiff has falsified evidence or court papers or made fraudulent statements to the Copyright Office in order to secure a copyright registration.

Another defense sometimes used is that the plaintiff has engaged in unfair competi-

tive practices in violation of antitrust laws. For example, if the plaintiff has refused to license certain highly marketable products unless they are "tied in" with licenses for less desirable products, the plaintiff may have misused the copyright in violation of unfair competition laws; such misuse will bar the plaintiff's case.

COMMENCING AN INFRINGEMENT SUIT
Civil copyright complaints must be filed within three years after the infringement takes place. This statute of limitations is absolute, and once the three-year period has elapsed, your copyright remedies may expire forever.

Please note that the plaintiff usually cannot argue that the three-year period begins only when he first discovered the infringement. However, if the defendant conceals the infringement or deceives the plaintiff into believing that infringement is not occurring, then the three-year period may begin to run only when the plaintiff actually discovers the infringement or when he reasonably should have discovered it. Moreover, there is some case law saying that, if any recent infringements occur within three years before the copyright action is commenced, the action will still be valid, even if the first infringing activities occurred many years before.

An action is *commenced* when the complaint is filed with a court of competent jurisdiction which is an appropriate United States District Court.

Where to File
The federal courts have *exclusive* jurisdiction over copyright infringement actions. Thus, even if yours is only a very small case, you can't sue on your copyright in the local small claims court. You have to file the complaint with a United States District Court.

However, not every lawsuit involving a copyright is considered a copyright infringement action. For example, if someone promises to transfer a copyright but breaks the promise, a breach of contract rather than an infringement, has occurred, and even though it involves a copyright, a state court action will be appropriate. The same is true if you license your rights but the licensee fails to pay royalties as agreed. Even disputes as to who owns a copyright don't necessarily result in cases that must be brought in federal court.

You must bring suit in the judicial districts where the defendant or his agent "resides" or may be "found." In other words, you have to prove that the defendant or the defendant's agent lives or does business in the district.

A person is *found* in a judicial district if she has certain minimal business contacts with that district—for instance, if the defendant owns real property or has business offices, sales agents, or numerous customers in the judicial district.

Under this rule, an *agent* is someone acting under the authority of a defendant. For example, an agent might be a subsidiary company, a sales manager for a company, or perhaps even a partner in a partnership.

You probably will want to bring the lawsuit in your home district. Thus you will do everything possible to prove that the defendant and/or the defendant's agent reside or do business in the district. If you can't do this, then you must usually sue in another judicial district.

If only one of many defendants resides in your judicial district, you will face additional problems in that you may have to bring suits in different districts in order to have proper venue with respect to all defendants.

Registration

As mentioned earlier, you must register the copyright and mention the registration in your complaint before you can bring the lawsuit, with one exception. If the Register of Copyrights refuses to issue a certificate but you believe you are entitled to it, you may commence the action if you give notice of it, with a copy of the complaint, to the Register of Copyrights. Your notice gives the Register the opportunity to intervene in the action and contest the registrability of the copyright claim.

Often you will be caught flatfooted without a registration when a significant infringement has occurred. Because registration certificates may take months to issue, the only remedy is to expedite the registration through what the Copyright Office calls *special handling*. This special procedure is designed to get a registration within a week or two, but like every rush job, it costs more (currently two hundred dollars extra—a filing fee). Special handling should always be handled by an attorney.

Settlement

Copyright actions are expensive. If you are considering a suit, try to settle without going to court unless the potential award of profits is very large, you are entitled to collect attorney's fees and statutory damages, or your case appears foolproof. The reason I encourage settlement is that infringement cases are difficult to win. First, you must prove that you are the copyright owner, and doing this may be difficult for works created by two or more people. Also, ownership is often complicated by factors such as publication without notice. Second, you have to prove that the defendant actually copied. Third, you have to overcome various defenses, especially fair use. Fourth, and most important, to establish profits, you must prove the defendant's gross revenues, and even when you do, the defendant usually proves so many deductions that the net profits, especially after apportionment, are minimal.

As a defendant, you should also consider settlement, particularly if the plaintiff is a prior registrant and entitled to attorney's fees and statutory damages. If you lose such a case, the court can award the full amount of statutory damages, up to $50,000 for each infringement committed willfully. Moreover, for any willful infringement for commercial gain, you may face criminal prosecution, although criminal copyright proceedings are rarely brought.

I encourage most defendants in copyright cases to make a *statutory offer of compro-*

mise, a procedure where the defendant makes a written settlement offer to the plaintiff, filed with the court. If the plaintiff rejects the offer but fails to recover more than the offered settlement amount, the plaintiff will pay the costs of the action. The defendant should offer an amount just slightly above the most probable recovery for the plaintiff. Most plaintiffs will strongly consider settlement where the offer is reasonable, saving both sides the time and expense of a trial.

INTERNATIONAL AND FOREIGN PROTECTION

American artists should be concerned about foreign and international protection when they publish their works abroad, when others copy their works abroad, and when they copy the works of foreign nationals.

The following is a very brief discussion of foreign and international copyright protection.

Foreign Protection

Generally speaking—and I mean *generally*—copyright protection abroad extends to literary, artistic, musical, dramatic, and audiovisual works. The rights protected are comparable to those under United States law, although the right to display is not generally recognized in foreign jurisdictions. The norm of duration appears to be life of the author plus fifty years.

In general, foreign protection requires few formalities. The United States is virtually unique in requiring copyright notices and registrations.

Works enjoy protection in a foreign country if first published there. Thus, you're more likely to secure a copyright in a foreign country if you first publish there rather than in the U.S.

To ensure foreign protection, you should comply with the guidelines of the Universal Copyright Convention, a treaty to which the United States and most important foreign countries are parties. The Universal Copyright Convention says that those who publish their works with proper copyright notices—consisting of the copyright symbol, the name of the copyright owner, and the year date of first publication—will be excused from complying with formalities prescribed by any treaty country.

The Universal Copyright Convention does not totally prescribe how you will be protected in a treaty country. It merely says that once you have used the appropriate copyright notice, you will enjoy the same protection as that country's own citizens first publishing their works in that country.

It's also possible to get foreign protection based on the Berne Convention, a treaty *not* subscribed to by the United States. To secure protection, you must either publish your work first in a Berne country or else publish it in a Berne country simultaneously with its publication in a non-Berne country.

Under another treaty, the Buenos Aires Convention, United States nationals who publish works fulfilling the formalities required in the United States and using the phrase "All Rights Reserved"—or some equivalent, like "Derechos Reservados"—on all published copies of the work will enjoy protection in all treaty countries.

Stopping Infringement Abroad

With a United States copyright, you can't stop people from committing acts abroad that would otherwise constitute copyright infringement. For example, if someone reproduces your work in the Netherlands, you can't use your United States copyright against that person. But when the infringing activities take place in part within the United States, you can use United States laws. Thus, if someone reproduces your work in the Netherlands and then imports and sells copies in the United States, you will have a valid claim under United States copyright law. The same is true if the work is reproduced in the United States and then shipped abroad for further distribution.

Whenever someone commits copyright infringement in a foreign country where you have protection, you can make a claim in the courts of that country. But sometimes you can also begin a lawsuit in the United States and in a particular judicial district, *if* you can establish personal jurisdiction over the defendant. For instance, if the defendant does business in the United States, it may be possible to bring your suit in the United States District Court for that judicial district and litigate your rights under foreign laws. The court will apply the foreign laws and not United States copyright law.

Copying Foreign Works

Many artists are concerned about copying works created or published abroad. If the works are not protected under United States law, then you can copy these works freely in the United States. For works protected in the United States, foreign artists do not enjoy any greater protection in the United States than do American artists, even if their own countries allow them more extended terms of protection. For example, if the foreign artist neglected to use a copyright notice, even if the notice were not required in his home country, in most cases the work would be in the public domain in the United States.

I recommend that when making decisions about copying foreign works you always consult an attorney because there are so many tricky cases involving foreign publications.

COPYRIGHT AS DISTINGUISHED FROM OTHER RIGHTS

Many times artists rely on copyright laws but are disappointed because not everything created by an artist is copyrightable. Often an artist must resort to other laws, such as those concerning patents and other trademarks.

Patent Laws

Since copyright laws do not protect the utilitarian aspects of works, you should turn to patent law to protect mechanical or utilitarian aspects of your work.

The two principal types of patents are *design patents* and *utility patents.*

Design patents apply to designs for articles of manufacture and protect the shapes and configurations of the articles. For example, although fabric designs usually are protectable under copyright law, garment designs usually are not. That is, the pictorial patterning on a piece of cloth can be considered artwork, but usually the shape of the garment is not copyrightable because clothing is considered utilitarian. The same is true for most modern furniture designs. So, to protect those designs, you generally apply for design patents.

The requirements for design patents include *novelty, originality,* and *nonobviousness.* You must also show that the design is *ornamental* and not primarily for functional or utilitarian purposes. To show novelty, you establish that the design has never been made before; to establish originality, you show that you haven't copied someone else. The design is nonobvious when a person with ordinary skill in the art would not have perceived it as obvious given prior art. To claim ornamentality, you show that the design is the product of aesthetic skill and artistic conception.

Most artists are not often involved with utility patents. Typically, utility patents relate to machines, devices, processes, articles of manufacture, compositions of matter, and other feats of engineering. But if you invent something new, you might need to rely on this type of patent. The requirements for a utility patent are somewhat similar: you have to show novelty, originality, and nonobviousness, as well as, of course, usefulness.

A few cautions: Compared to copyright applications, patent applications are much more expensive and time-consuming. Also, you should use a licensed patent attorney. In addition, getting the patent issued is a must. You have no protection until there is an issued patent, and you can't sit on your hands while your invention languishes. The patent laws require prompt applications, and the first person to the Patent Office often becomes the patent owner, even though two or more inventors are still squabbling as to who invented first.

Protecting Ideas

Although copyright law does not protect ideas, there is protection based not on the sanctity of ideas but rather on the sanctity of certain relationships.

For example, within a contractual relationship, ideas can be protected. The best form of idea protection is a *written contract* providing that a disclosed idea will not be used or further communicated by someone to whom you disclose the idea.

Next best is an *oral agreement*. The problem, of course, is proving the agreement because it's your word against someone else's. If you are going to have an oral agreement, then have witnesses present to substantiate it.

Another form of protection is an *implied agreement*. Even though the parties do not openly agree to anything, an implied agreement comes about if the circumstances of the transaction show that there must have been an understanding. For instance, if you ask for food at a restaurant, there is no express agreement that you are going to pay for it. However, try walking out without paying. You have to pay because there is an implied agreement to do so.

The same can be true for ideas. One way to create the circumstances for an implied agreement is to send a query letter asking whether the person would be interested in receiving the idea for purposes of examination only. If she indicates that she wants you to submit the idea—and you want to get this indication in writing—then you have an implied understanding that she will not use or communicate your idea without your permission and, if she does, she will pay you a reasonable sum for the value of the idea.

Sometimes the relationship between the parties may allow protection. Ideas disclosed within the context of attorney-client, doctor-patient, psychotherapist-patient, and preacher-penitent relationships can be protected. The presumption is that ideas disclosed within such relationships are revealed in confidence, and the law will pre-vent the breach of the confidential relationship and protect the idea.

Sometimes within the context of certain business relationships, ideas can be protected. For instance, ideas confidentially disclosed to partners and other business associates may be protected under some circumstances.

Any time you disclose an idea—even to a lawyer or a preacher—you should mention that you are doing so in confidence.

Unfair Competition

Under the heading *unfair competition* is a broad body of law that can protect ideas, information, and materials.

For example, some kinds of wrongful misappropriation may constitute actionable unfair competition. A competitor who enters your premises unlawfully, rifles through your files, and steals undisclosed information and art materials, can be enjoined from using what he takes.

Unfair competition law also protects trade secrets. Basically, a trade secret is valuable information or materials used in one's business that are not known by or made generally available to the public, and that are maintained in secrecy. Trade secrets sometimes comprise customer lists, business know-how, sources of supplies and materials, secret processes, and like information. An absolute requirement is that the trade secret owner take appropriate measures to maintain secrecy, including contracts with employees requiring secrecy.

If protection is available, you can block employees and competitors from using trade secrets unlawfully misappropriated. Please note, however, that once the secret is lawfully disclosed, protection is usually lost, and anyone who deciphers the secret can use it. For example, if you have a secret customer list developed after years of effort, someone else could contact the very same customers and compile a competitive list if the names were readily available from the phone book and other public domain sources. The same is true of secret processes. Many artists have special ways of doing things that they teach their employees. Former employees who start businesses on their own may legitimately use the same techniques learned from the employer if these secrets can be learned from a book.

Trademarks and Service Marks

As mentioned earlier, words and titles are not copyrightable. The same may be true for simple geometric logos, because copyright law requires some minimal creativity before it will confer protection. But if the word, title, or logo is used in commerce as a trademark or service mark, it may be protected under trademark and unfair competition laws.

A *trademark* is a word, symbol, name, insignia, logo, phrase, configuration, or other device used to identify your goods and distinguish them from those made or sold by others. A *service mark* is the same type of device, but it is designed to identify your services and distinguish them from the services of others.

Typically, the trademark is used on labels, tags, and packaging materials for the goods or is directly printed on the goods themselves; the service mark is generally printed on business cards, stationery, business signs, and advertising materials such as leaflets and brochures.

Generally speaking, the first one to use a trademark or service mark in a geographic territory will own that mark in the territory, provided that person makes a continuous and substantial use of the mark in the territory. However, you must register your mark in order to perfect your rights. A system of federal registration administered by the United States Patent and Trademark Office in Washington, D.C., is parallel to systems of trademark registration in the fifty states. Each state has its own registration system.

Bear in mind that you can register a trademark or service mark only after you've used it. Many times, of course, the artist is not using the logo or trademark he or she created; the client is using the mark and usually becomes the trademark owner. With trademarks, it is *use* that confers ownership.

Registration is not always necessary and not always possible for words, insignias, and other devices used as trademarks or service marks. For example, registration may be refused for surnames, descriptive terms, and even misdescriptive terms. Nonetheless, even some marks initially unprotectable can still claim protection under the law of unfair competition. For example, a descriptive term (such as *Speedy* for a delivery service) can be protected and perhaps even registered if it attains *secondary meaning.*

Unregistered marks can still claim protection under the law of unfair competition. Generally speaking, if an unregistered mark or other indication of source or origin obtains secondary meaning, then the law sometimes confers protection. Secondary meaning is present when, because of substantial advertising and use, the mark or other device has become closely associated in the public's mind with the merchant, manufacturer, or provider of services. Keep in mind, of course, that secondary meaning is often achieved only after years of use and advertising.

Moral Rights

A few states, such as California, Massachusetts, and New York, now have statutes protecting artists' moral rights. These laws are designed to protect works of art from mutilation or alteration, and allow the artist more control in how the work is used and credited. See Chapter 2 for a full discussion of moral-rights laws.

CONCLUSION

The courts have interpreted the copyright laws in thousands of reported decisions, and it is impossible to give you all the details. Thus, I've only touched on the most salient aspects of copyright law as represented by the copyright legislation itself.

Nonetheless, if you read the statutes and review what I have said, at least you should understand the essentials of copyright law.

Nothing said here can substitute for an attorney's advice on a case-by-case basis. Remember that each transaction is unique and requires special attention and knowledge. Thus, I recommend an attorney's advice for all important transactions.

Of course, unless you can afford an attorney to handle all copyright transactions, you will have to make some day-to-day decisions yourself. You may not always have an attorney tell you what date to put on a copyright notice, what works are made for hire, what works are public domain, and so on. You may deal with dozens or even hundreds of works each week, and you can't always consult an attorney about every one of them. Therefore, I recommend that you secure general advice from a copyright attorney about all the day-to-day decisions regarding copyrights and that you further secure from the attorney copyright-related forms that you can use in all your transactions. Such forms include licensing agreements, invoices and order forms for clients commissioning work from you, work-made-for-hire agreements, and copyright transfer agreements.

Now that documents are put on computer, you can store standard agreements on your computer and adjust them for each separate transaction.

Remember that copyrights are valuable not only in connection with individual works but also in relation to your business in its entirety. When you take on a partner or sell your business, the value of the business may be partially determined by the copyrights you own. The more you protect your copyrights, the more valuable your business will be.

Finally, preventive law is always better than crisis law. Fifty dollars worth of your time learning about copyright law is much better than $5,000 of your time frantically running around to resolve a situation that would not have occurred had you known what you were doing. In the same light, $100 spent on attorney's fees to do something right is much better than $10,000 spent on litigation.

COPYRIGHTS AND COMPUTER-GENERATED ARTWORK

By Roger A. Gilcrest

The use of computer technology to create works of art presents some difficult issues pertaining to copyright protection. Many of these questions can be answered by looking to the standards and rules just discussed, but this section deals with how some of the major copyright issues relate to computer-generated or computer-enhanced artistic works.

ORIGINALITY

Computer-generated artwork includes works produced or enhanced by a computer, such as computer drawings or computer animation. These works can fulfill the requirement that the work be original even though the artist's medium may have been the computer keyboard (or the commonly used mouse) and the computer screen rather than the brushes and palettes more historically associated with artists. So long as the creation was that of the artist and contains no copying, it may be protected under copyright law. Conversely, works that are merely the result of skillful copying—such as the rendering of an earlier work into a form that can be displayed on a computer—even though the result of expertise in the computer field, are not protected, because they lack originality.

Between the two extremes of completely

Roger A. Gilcrest advises artists, writers, and musicians on legal matters as the acting chairman of the Lawyers for the Arts in Cincinnati, Ohio. He is an attorney with Frost & Jacobs, specializing in intellectual property law, particularly patents, trademarks, and copyrights. He received his J.D. from the University of San Diego.

original works and simple copies are works that are new renderings of earlier works, such as one altered by use of a computer's ability to change aspects of the earlier work. In these cases, originality becomes a question of degree. Most courts have applied the rule that any "distinguishable variation" will be considered to have the required degree of originality so long as such variation is the product of the artist's independent efforts and is more than trivial.

Suppose, for example, that an artist produces, based on an earlier two-dimensional work, a fully three-dimensional rendering that would allow the viewer to "travel within" the work itself. In such a case, the artist certainly used much of the original work but most probably would have embellished upon it to an extent that the newly created computer work would be considered original.

It is important to emphasize here that copyright law does not protect ideas or methods, but only expressions. Therefore the idea to produce art by use of a computer in a certain way, or the method of doing so, is not protected by copyright. Rather, only tangible results of these methods that fulfill the other copyright requirements can be protected. For instance, a method of rendering a drawing into an artistic needlework by the use of computer-guided machinery is not copyrightable. The law of patents or trade secrets must be used for this type of protection. However, the individual artwork so produced could be protected by copyright so long as it met all the other legal requirements of a copyrightable work.

FIXING THE WORK

As we have seen, a work must be fixed to qualify as copyrightable subject matter, that is, the work must be rendered to a tangible form. For computer art, works may be fixed by using the various computer-readable tapes and disks commonly available today.

THE COPYRIGHT NOTICE

When a computer-generated work is "published"—by methods such as the sale of the computer program disk or the printout containing the artwork—the proper copyright notice must be placed on the work to protect the owner's rights. The purpose of the notice is to inform the public that rights to the work are reserved to the copyright claimant rather than being placed in the public domain by publication.

Copyright notices for computer-generated art are the same as those for any work. They must contain three elements: (1) the familiar symbol © (or the word *Copyright* or the abbreviation *Copr.* in the United States); (2) the name of the copyright claimant (either the author or anyone otherwise having obtained rights to the work); and (3) the year of first publication of the work. Additional dates can be added to subsequent editions of the work as they are produced and published.

There is no strict rule regarding where the copyright notice must be placed. It should, however, be visible to the naked eye and should be placed so as to be reasonably easily seen. For computer-generated works, the notice may be placed on the disk or tape holding the computer program or may be incorporated into the computer-screen display of the artwork. For instance, for computer animation, the notice is normally placed at either the beginning or the end of the animation sequence.

DEPOSIT OF THE COPYRIGHTED WORK FOR REGISTRATION

The rules of the Copyright Office require that at least one copy of the artistic work be provided with the application for registration. For computer-generated artwork, pictures or drawings of the artwork may be used as deposit copies. In the case of computer animations, drawings, photographs, or videotapes of the work may be deposited with the application. Printouts of the screen displays can also be used.

INFRINGEMENT

Copyright law has kept pace with technology in its definition of *copy* for the purposes of showing that someone has infringed another's copyright. The definition of *copy* includes any material objects by which a work may be "perceived, reproduced or otherwise communicated, either directly or with the aid of a machine or a device." If, for instance, a copyrighted work is input into a computer's memory, it would be considered to have been copied and the artist's or author's copyright thereby infringed. For example, if a computer-generated animation were copied and distributed in the form of computer-readable floppy disks, infringement would occur.

A SAMPLE AGREEMENT

An agreement for licensing computer artwork follows. It establishes precisely what rights are being licensed, how and when the artist will be paid, and how long the agreement will last.

CONCLUSION

While many of the questions regarding copyrighting computer-generated artwork can be answered by reference to established copyright law, new issues such as originality must be resolved by careful application of copyright principles to these new technologies.

Other areas, such as the placement of the copyright notice and the deposit of copies for registration purposes, are more questions of practicality; they pertain to fulfilling the requirements of the Copyright Act and the rules and regulations of the Copyright Office.

Specific questions regarding Copyright Office requirements can be answered by calling the Public Information Division of the Copyright Office or by consulting your attorney.

COMPUTER ART AGREEMENT

This Agreement is entered into between [Artist's Name] ("Licensor") of [Artist's Address] and [Licensee's Name] of [Licensee's Address] ("Licensee") (hereinafter collectively referred to as "the Parties").

WHEREAS, Licensor has created an artistic work entitled [Title of Work] (the "Work") which is capable of being displayed through the use of a computer or other computer-driven or computer-enhanced audio, visual, or audio-visual device, and which is the subject of U.S. Copyright Registration No. [insert number].

WHEREAS, Licensor desires to grant, and Licensee desires to obtain, a license to reproduce and publish the Work upon the terms and conditions agreed to between the Parties.

NOW, THEREFORE, in view of the foregoing, the Parties agree as follows:

I. LICENSE GRANT

Licensor hereby grants to Licensee a nonexclusive [or exclusive] license to reproduce and sell, rent, or otherwise publish directly or through others a total of [Insert Number] [e.g., up to fifteen thousand (15,000)] copies of the Work per year within the United States [or other geographical limitation], whether such copies are in computer-readable or non-computer-readable form, including without limitation computer disks, computer tapes, and other forms of computer money, video tape, and film [add others where appropriate].

II. ROYALTY

Licensee shall pay to Licensor an amount equal to [insert amount] dollars ([amount numerical]) [e.g., two dollars ($2.00)] for each such copy so reproduced during the term of this Agreement.

III. TERMS OF PAYMENT

The Royalty shall be payable [insert time] [e.g., monthly, quarterly, yearly] based upon the number of copies so reproduced during each successive period, and payment shall be made at the end of each successive period.

IV. RECORDS

Licensee shall keep accurate and current records of the number of copies so reproduced and shall make such records available to Licensor upon written request. Each payment of royalty to Licensor shall include a statement of the number of copies made during the period for which payment has been made and the total number of copies made to the date of such statement.

V. COPYRIGHT

Licensor shall retain the exclusive copyright to the Work and nothing in this Agreement shall be construed to affect Licensor's exclusivity to such rights.

VI. TERM OF AGREEMENT

This Agreement shall be effective for a period of [insert time period] [e.g., three (3)] years from the date of its execution.

VII. INTEGRATION CLAUSE

This written agreement constitutes the entire agreement between the Parties.

AGREED:

_____
[Licensor's Name]

_____
[Licensee's Name]

0368C

COMMONLY ASKED QUESTIONS: COPYRIGHTS

Q. *Do I have to put a copyright notice on my work if it appears in a magazine?*

A. Not necessarily. The notice for the magazine issue, usually found in the masthead, protects the entire contents of the issue, except for advertising materials not placed by the publisher. However, if you do not have your notice on the work as it appears in the magazine, a third person may take a license from the magazine owner to use your work, and that third party may have a defense against you unless you had previously registered your copyright in the work.

Q. *Since I'm just a hobbyist and do not intend to sell my work, do I have to put a copyright notice on my work?*

A. Only copies of *published* works need to bear a copyright notice. Therefore, if you never distribute, sell, transfer, lend, lease, or rent your work or copies of it, you need not use a copyright notice. If you merely show your work to others, it does not need to bear a copyright notice. If you're in doubt about whether the work would be deemed published, put a notice on it anyway.

Q. *I published some artwork in a magazine and was paid in complimentary copies. Has the magazine bought any of my rights?*

A. The Copyright Act requires written, signed instruments in order to effect a transfer of exclusive rights. However, nonexclusive licenses and permissions can be granted orally. In the absence of a written agreement, if a work is published in a magazine with the consent of the artist, the presumption is that the publisher has acquired only a nonexclusive right to reproduce and distribute the artwork as part of the magazine issue, any revision of the issue, or any later issue of the magazine.

Q. *I published an illustration in a university's literary magazine. Two years later, I saw the illustration on a poster and a brochure. I was paid only for the magazine. What can I do?*

A. You should request an additional payment for these unauthorized uses. If you feel more strongly, or if payment is not forthcoming after making the request, you can sue for copyright infringement. After all, if the understanding was that the license extended only to the magazine use, the uses on a poster and a brochure were outside the scope of the license.

Q. *I have designed a typeface. Do I hold a copyright to it?*

A. The weight of authority is that there is no copyright protection for typeface designs. Nonetheless, it is possible to imagine highly ornate designs that might qualify for protection even if used incidentally as typeface designs.

Q. *I am considering doing some clip art. Can I retain any rights to it?*

A. As a practical matter, since your clip art is intended to be widely used by persons not seeking permissions, it may be difficult to enforce a copyright in clip art. It is possible to create clip art, send it out with copyright notices, require that all users promise in writing to use your copyright notice in connection with it, and thus maintain protection, but it is not always practical to do so.

Q. *I sold a design to a greeting card company. I sold all rights for the design to be used on greeting cards only. However, two years later, I found my design on mugs, notecards, and even pens—products put out by another company. I thought my de-*

sign could be reproduced only on greeting cards. What happened? What can I do?

A. Clearly the other company is engaged in copyright infringement. However, if the other company received permission from the greeting card company to use your design, you could have problems unless you had a prior copyright registration for the work. If the greeting card company did give the other company permission, you may have a direct action against the greeting card company for copyright infringement. You probably should ask for additional payment for the unauthorized uses, and if not forthcoming, make a claim for copyright infringement and unfair competition.

Q. *I sent samples of a design for a line of dresses to a manufacturer of women's clothing. The manufacturer never responded to my query. A year later, I looked through the racks of a local department store and saw a dress that was designed exactly like my sketches. I know this is my design. What can I do? What should I do in the future when submitting ideas?*

A. Statutory copyright protection usually is not available for dress designs. Garments are considered useful articles, and copyright protection in the design of a useful article is available only to the extent that it "incorporates pictorial, graphic, or sculptural features that can be identified separately from and are capable of existing independently of, the utilitarian aspects of the article." Another reason is that copyright protection for utilitarian works extends only to copying for purposes of explanation but not to copying for purposes of use.

Therefore, a copyright in a dress design can be used against someone who duplicates the design on paper to be used to show other fabric designers how to dupli-

cate the design but can't be used to prevent others from actually embodying the design in clothing. You probably have no recourse against the clothing manufacturer.

If you want protection for clothing designs, it is best to use nondisclosure agreements, or, at the very least, set up your transactions so that the designs are disclosed in confidence and that the other party is legally obligated to maintain confidentiality. Another possibility is a design patent.

Q. *I am frequently asked to modify scientific and medical illustrations. I start with a drawing someone else has done and then I change it. Do I give the original artist credit? Is it okay if I completely redraw the figure and change it?*

A. If the work you're using is subject to copyright protection, then you are engaged in copyright infringement, since you are preparing a derivative work without consent. It is possible that you may have a fair use defense, and giving the original artist credit will work in your favor in establishing fair use. However, if you change the drawing, you cannot just give a simple credit to the artist; you should probably indicate that your work is "based on" or is a "changed version of" the original work, because if you do not make this careful distinction, you are falsely crediting the original artist with a work that is not his or hers.

Merely by redrawing the figure and changing it, you do not escape liability if it can be proved that you were copying from the original work.

Q. *I often get my inspirations from clippings I have collected from magazines. Is this okay?*

A. Because copyright protection does not extend to ideas, if you are only using your inspirations, you will probably be all right. On the other hand, to the extent that you copy the actual expression of works taken from magazines, you may be engaged in copyright infringement.

Q. *Do I have to title every painting in order to get it copyrighted?*

A. No. However, the copyright registration forms usually ask for a title of the work. Theoretically, you could put in a title of the work in the registration form and yet not actually put a title on the work, but I don't recommend this.

Q. *In art class my instructor told me to put a copyright symbol on a painting I copied from another work. Is this right?*

A. Yes and no. Because the copy is probably a derivative work, it has its own copyright and can have its own notice. However, if the work you copied was not your own and is subject to copyright protection, then you may have committed an infringement. Thus, putting your notice on the copy will only invite further problems and claims for unfair competition.

In addition, if your notice misleads the public as to the identity of the original work, you may have problems with moral rights laws as well.

Q. *About fifteen years ago, the local historical society commissioned me to do some sketches of historical homes around the city; the society was going to use them for promotional purposes. They are still handing out the prints, even though the first edition has run out. Who holds the copyright? Can I ask for payment for further editions?*

A. Assuming you were an independent contractor, you still hold the copyright unless you transferred it away in writing. If your understanding was that the historical society had the right to use only the first print run, then you may be entitled to payment for further editions.

Q. *Should I put my copyright notice on the slides and photographs of my work that I send to galleries and potential clients?*

A. Absolutely. There is every possibility that by sending your works out to galleries and potential clients you are meeting the criteria for publishing the work, thus requiring the use of copyright notices.

Q. *Once I give permission to an art director to reproduce my work, can he change it without my permission?*

A. If you have given permission only to reproduce your work, then no one else has the right to change it. However, in many advertising-related transactions, there is an implied agreement permitting the art director to make some changes in order to conform to the client's wishes. If you want to prevent changes, you may need to get it in writing.

Q. *I am a sign painter. Can I copyright my signs?*

A. Yes and no. If there is true artwork in the sign—meeting the standard of being "an original work of authorship," as explained on pages 2-3—then that artwork can be protected as a pictorial work. If the sign contains a significant amount of literary material, there may be protection for a literary work. However, this is usually not the case, because most signs incorporate merely names, titles, or short phrases that are not protected.

9. *If I am not registered at the Copyright Office, can I still put my notice on my work?*

A. Absolutely. In fact, you should use your notice on all copies of published works.

EASY REFERENCE CHECK-LISTS: COPYRIGHTS

To be copyrightable, artwork must be:
- [ ] Original, a work you created without copying or plagiarizing
- [ ] Fixed on paper, canvas, or some other tangible medium
- [ ] A work with at least minimal creativity or artistic content

Some types of artwork that can be copyrighted:
- [ ] Illustrations used in advertisements
- [ ] Magazine and book illustrations
- [ ] Drawings and paintings
- [ ] Etchings, engravings, woodcuts, and silkscreens
- [ ] Cartoons and comic strips
- [ ] Posters
- [ ] Product labels with designs
- [ ] Scientific drawings
- [ ] Architectural renderings

What can't be copyrighted:
- [ ] Ideas
- [ ] Utilitarian works
- [ ] United States government works, such as forms

Copyright registration requires sending:
- [ ] The filled-in application form (usually form VA)
- [ ] A deposit copy(s) of the work
- [ ] A money order or check for ten dollars, payable to the Register of Copyrights
- [ ] A cover letter explaining your request

Deposit copies:
- [ ] As a general rule, send one copy for unpublished works, two for published works.
- [ ] One copy is sufficient for greeting cards, post cards, stationery, labels, advertisements, scientific drawings, and globes.
- [ ] Send transparencies or prints in most cases.
- [ ] Use color transparencies or prints if your work is in color.
- [ ] For limited, numbered editions, send one copy or identifying reproductions.

Some types of reproduction rights:
- [ ] First rights, where the buyer can reproduce your work only once, but is the first to do so
- [ ] One-time rights, where the buyer can reproduce your work only once
- [ ] Reprint rights, where the buyer can publish your work after it has already appeared elsewhere

CHAPTER 2

MORAL RIGHTS AND GOOD BUSINESS PRACTICES

By David M. Spatt

You are an artist producing graphic art for commercial use and reproduction, or creating artworks for exhibition, sale, or your own enjoyment. As such, you are entitled to certain rights you may not be aware of. In this chapter, I'll explain the rights to which you are entitled and how to obtain them. I'll also show you how to avoid certain business practices that can, at best, be very frustrating, and, at worst, cause substantial damage.

This chapter is not intended to replace sound legal advice regarding specific situations, since each decision you make will require a different treatment. When you are faced with a complex legal or business decision, you should consult a competent arts attorney, an artist's rep, or another artist who has negotiated agreements to her advantage.

Your rights as a creator are protected to some extent by various federal and state laws. In situations where the laws don't provide enough protection, you must protect your rights through the proper use of contract language in a written contract.

When you're entering a contractual relationship, the rights discussed here will be points of negotiation. You don't have to

David M. Spatt, a graduate of the University of Rhode Island and Brooklyn Law School, is an attorney specializing in arts and entertainment. His New York and Rhode Island practice has been based in Narrangansett, Rhode Island, since 1981, where his clientele encompasses visual artists, theater companies, writers, and musicians, as well as nonprofit organizations located in the northeast. He is founding director of the Ocean State Lawyers for the Arts. He also lectures regularly at the Rhode Island School of Design about the legal aspects of art.

turn down a job simply because your client, or others with whom you are dealing, won't accept everything discussed in this chapter. You must weigh your needs and those of your client to reach a fair compromise.

MORAL RIGHTS

In 1958, an Alexander Calder black-and-white mobile was donated for placement in the Pittsburgh Airport. The Allegheny County Department of Aviation repainted the mobile green and gold, locked it in place, and motorized it. Even though the work was being presented in a manner contrary to the artist's intentions, Calder was helpless because there was no legal protection for an artist's moral rights at the time.

Moral rights, or *droit moral*, is a concept of European origin designed to help artists protect their works and their reputations. It has only recently begun to gain acceptance in the United States. A few states have passed moral rights laws, and these rights can also be enforced through contracts.

Moral rights generally fall into three categories: the right of creation, the right of paternity, and the right of integrity.

The Right of Creation

You have the right to create or destroy your work. You also have the right to control publication or disclosure of your work.

You may think that protection of this right is unnecessary since, while your work is in your possession, you have total control. Consider what would happen, though, if you created a painting with which you were not satisfied and threw it away, only to have a stranger find your discarded work, restore it, and sell it as an original work of art with your name on it. Your right of creation would enable you to get the work back so that it could be completely destroyed.

Some states have enacted moral rights laws that include protection of the right of creation. The Copyright Act may also provide some protection, as would proposed

posed federal moral rights legislation.

Unfortunately, it is practically impossible to protect this right by contract usage. The time when you would exercise the right of creation is before any contract would exist.

The Right of Paternity

As the creator of a work of art, it is important for you to be credited with the creation, or authorship, of that work. If you sell reproduction rights to a greeting card company, for example, and 10,000 cards are distributed with your work of art displayed on the front, having your name included as the artist may go a long way toward acquainting the public with your name. The right of paternity would guarantee that your name would be included on every copy of your work, even after you no longer owned or possessed it.

Conversely, if someone credited you as the artist of a work, you could disclaim your authorship if you were not in fact involved or if the work was yours but had been altered to a certain degree.

A well-known case involving the right of paternity arose when Antonio Vargas sued *Esquire* magazine. Vargas created the famous series of "Varga Girls" for *Esquire*. After his contract expired, *Esquire* continued to run the series as the "Esquire Girls" and denied Vargas credit for the works. Vargas lost his legal battle, but the right of paternity, if it had been available, would have allowed a more favorable result.

The right of paternity has been included in some state legislation, such as the New York Arts and Cultural Affairs Law and the California Civil Code. These laws give the right to claim, or disclaim, the authorship of works of "fine art." It can also be protected through contract language.

An example of a contract clause to protect your right of paternity to the extent of guaranteeing an artist's credit could read:

> Company shall include [insert artist's name or pseudonym] on all copies of the work prepared herein.

The Right of Integrity

As the creator of artwork, it is important to prevent others from altering, mutilating, or destroying your art without your consent. The right of integrity would allow you to stop others from changing or destroying your work even if you no longer owned it.

The right of integrity is the moral right of most concern to artists, and it is the subject of more extensive state legislation than the rights of creation or paternity.

In 1972, the executor of sculptor David Smith's estate had the paint stripped from several of Smith's works. It was the executor's belief that the stripping would improve the works. If the right of integrity had been available at the time, it would have provided an arts group with the means to prevent the alterations and protect the artist's original intent. The right of integrity also would have given Calder a means of preventing the alteration of his mobile by the Allegheny County Department of Aviation.

The basis for this right is that a work that is altered is not an expression of your true creative intent. Also, you should have a right to protect your reputation, and unauthorized modifications present a work falsely, allowing potential damage to your reputation.

You may protect your right of integrity to some extent by using the following contract provision:

> Company agrees that neither it, nor its assigns, shall damage, alter, or modify the work without prior written approval of the Artist. In the event Company, or its assigns, decide to destroy the work, it shall offer the Artist a reasonable opportunity to recover the work at no cost to the Artist except for an obligation to indemnify the Company for the amount by which the Company's cost of recovery exceeds the costs of the Company's proposed destruction.

Protecting Your Moral Rights

Federal legislation is being proposed that would give you certain moral rights, but, for the time being, only some of the states have passed moral rights laws. The California and New York laws are the most comprehensive.

New York protects the rights of paternity and integrity, although these rights are accorded only to works of *fine art*. That term appears to be broadly defined, although the definition will probably be applied on a case-by-case basis. Also, protection does not extend to work prepared under contract for advertising or trade use unless the contract so provides. (This is applicable to most graphic artists.) Further, any alteration or defacement of the work that is the result of regular negligence doesn't violate the New York statute. The artist's protection against damage is limited to that caused by gross negligence.

The previously mentioned contract provision will give you some protection for works that aren't covered by state statute or works that are prepared in a state without moral rights legislation. Unfortunately, without legislation, these contract clauses may be difficult, or impossible, to enforce against someone who purchases your work from the buyer who originally contracted with you. The second purchaser is not considered a party to the contract between you and the original purchaser and, therefore, is generally not bound by its provisions. As always, there are exceptions to this rule, but complex issues of contract law are involved, so you should consult an arts-law specialist in each particular case.

Moral rights legislation can bind subsequent purchasers of artwork and, at this time, has been enacted in the states of New York, California, Massachusetts, Rhode Island, Louisiana, Maine, New Jersey, and Pennsylvania, and has been proposed in other states and as a federal statute.

If you are unable to negotiate moral rights protection into a contract, you should not agree to expressly waive any post-sale rights in the project that may be applicable. Delete any contract clause that contains a statement such as:

> The Artist hereby waives all right to recover, restore, or object to alteration or destruction of the work herein, and she waives all rights to resale royalties or other post-sale rights, in the event said rights are granted by statute.

OTHER RIGHTS

Two other rights of the artist are beginning to gain acceptance, the right to resale royalties and rights related to consignment arrangements. Like moral rights, these rights can be protected by state law or by contract language.

Resale Royalties

If you produce an original work of art and sell it to a collector, there is a good chance that the collector will sell it at a substantial profit after your reputation has grown. In effect, the collector profits from your name and reputation, and you may believe you should be paid a percentage of the collector's profit. This percentage is called a *resale royalty*.

This concept is known as *droite de suite* and literally means that you have the right to follow your work and participate in the proceeds of resales. It differs from that of royalties under the Copyright Act as it applies only to resale of the original work of art, and copyright royalties are based upon the sale of reproductions of the work. *Droit de suite* would have limited applicability to the graphic artist, because the graphic artist deals more in reproduction rights than in original work.

California's statute is the only one that guarantees you resale royalties from subsequent sales of your work. Under its law, even if your work is resold three times after you sold it, you have the right to a percentage of the profits from these sales.

In other states, resale royalties can be incorporated into a contract as follows:

> Artist shall be entitled to _____ per-

cent of the proceeds from any subsequent sale of Artist's work by Company, and Company shall pay Artist said percentage within _____ days of said sale, and said payment shall include an accounting of the sale and payment.

As discussed earlier, contract provisions granting resale royalties bind only the purchaser who directly contracted with you. Subsequent purchasers generally won't be subject to its provisions.

Consignment Sales

Assume that you have created five paintings and you want to exhibit or sell them. You decide to place them with a dealer who will handle the exhibition or sale in return for a percentage of the proceeds. Two weeks later, you learn that your paintings were stolen from the dealer. Without a written agreement or protective legislation, the dealer may not be responsible for your loss.

You can make the dealer responsible by entering a consignment relationship. A consignment arrangement with a dealer or gallery protects you if the works are destroyed or stolen, the dealer or gallery goes out of business and creditors go after your artworks, or the works are sold and the dealer refuses to pay you. Properly used, a consignment agreement will require the gallery or dealer to safeguard your work from damage or loss of value, as well as guarantee that you will receive the proceeds from any sales.

You can create a consignment agreement through the use of a written agreement, examples of which are in Chapter 3.

In some states, you do not have to create a consignment relationship on your own—state laws do it for you. These laws generally state that delivery of your work to a dealer, who accepts it, automatically creates a consignment, unless the dealer pays you the full price of the work on acceptance. In such a consignment, the dealer holds your work, and proceeds from sales, in trust for you. Also, creditors of the dealer cannot take your work as payment for the dealer's debts. Finally, you would be entitled to pay-

ment of your percentage before the dealer's fee is paid.

Where the law creates the consignment, you may have several different remedies if the dealer fails to fulfill his obligations. You can sue for breach of contract, assuming you had one and can prove it. You can sue the dealer for a breach of the responsibilities created by the state consignment law. The dealer may even be subject to criminal violations, as would be the case in California.

Artist-dealer consignment laws currently exist, in one form or another, in the states of Arizona, Arkansas, California, Colorado, Connecticut, Florida, Idaho, Illinois, Iowa, Kentucky, Maryland, Massachusetts, Michigan, Minnesota, Missouri, Montana, New Mexico, New York, North Carolina, Ohio, Oregon, Pennsylvania, Tennessee, Texas, Washington, and Wisconsin.

BUSINESS PRACTICES

In addition to understanding your rights as an artist, you should realize that certain business situations can put you at an extreme disadvantage when dealing with clients and others. You should make every attempt to avoid these working relationships.

Working on Speculation

It would be unethical for a client to expect any professional to expend time and materials on a project that the client need not pay for. Working on speculation allows this situation to occur. The client will request that you work on a project, but payment will depend on the client's "satisfaction" or "acceptance." You, therefore, take the risk of working many hours without getting paid, putting yourself at a severe disadvantage.

This problem doesn't arise only when the whole project is done on speculation. If an agreement is reached that payment won't be made until the work is completed, but you have to prepare roughs for the client's approval, it's possible that you'll put in many hours on preliminary sketches just to have the client reject them and pull out of the agreement. Once again, you will have worked without compensation.

The possibility of working on speculation can be avoided by including a payment schedule in any agreement for your services. The schedule may provide that the client will pay you one-third of the fee upon signing the agreement, one-third on approval of preliminary drawings (if applicable), and the final third upon completion of the project, acceptance of which may not be unreasonably withheld by the client.

Billable Changes

A related issue arises when the client requests material changes in the project after work has begun. The agreement should state that any such changes will be billed to the client, in addition to the design fee, because the extra time to make the changes was not originally contemplated when both parties agreed to a fee for the project. Once again, by signing a properly drafted agreement, you will avoid the possibility of not being compensated for your time.

Buy-out of Rights

It is fundamental that an artist understand the value of her work to herself and to others. Many artists believe that when an artwork is created for a client, the client becomes the owner of that work. Fortunately for the knowledgeable artist, a transfer of rights is not that simple. Under the Copyright Act of 1976, each work involves a "bundle of rights," and any one or a number of those rights can be transferred to one client or many different clients.

An example of how the bundle-of-rights concept works is where a cartoonist creates a comic strip for use in a daily newspaper and the rights for the strip are purchased by a large syndicate. If the artist sells all of her rights to the syndicate (a *buy-out*), then the client has full control of the bundle of rights.

On the other hand, if the cartoonist reserved her other rights, she could sell the comic-book rights to another publisher, the television rights to an independent produc-

tion company, movie rights to a film producer, and other subsidiary rights to various toy companies for the design and manufacture of stuffed toys, plastic toys, board games, and video games.

If you reserve your rights, instead of realizing one fee, you can receive many payments, which, in some cases, will have the potential for future royalties.

You may think that your work doesn't have the potential for many future uses. The point is, if the work isn't that marketable, why does the original client want to buy out all the rights?

Other reasons not to sell all the rights at one time are worth considering. The client may not have any use for, or even want, the additional rights. A greeting card manufacturer may not be equipped to produce posters, so it doesn't need the poster rights. Conversely, the card company may want the poster rights and, in return, will pay you a percentage of poster sales as a royalty. Most artists will grab such an opportunity for additional revenue from their work, but be sure you don't transfer the extra rights without some extra thought. You should consider whether the card company is experienced in producing posters and, if so, whether the quality of the posters properly reproduced the artwork created by the artist. If the client does a poor job of creating your posters, the low quality may reflect on you and damage your reputation in the marketplace. Also, badly produced posters have little value, and your potential for royalty earnings will be substantially reduced.

Before granting rights to a client, consider the following questions: Is the client experienced in producing the product for which the right is granted? Is it experienced in marketing the product? If the client plans to assign the rights to another company that will produce or market the product, will your consent be required? If the client has experience, what is its track record? What do other artists who have dealt with the client say about its past performance?

Other questions arise when the client wants worldwide rights for a particular product. It may be experienced in distributing to the American market, but the European market would be another matter. If foreign distribution would be handled by a good foreign company licensed by the client, then the artist may feel secure in transferring the rights. *The key to a successful relationship is to know the client and its needs, and to agree to terms that will benefit everyone.*

If a client does buy out all of the reproduction rights, you should attempt to retain ownership of the original artwork. Your work may be a valuable commodity in the future when you have attained a reputation and a devoted following.

There is usually no reason to give this right away, although the client may demand the originals anyway. If the reason for such a demand is that the client wants to display the original in her offices, or to produce additional copies, you still need not give up ownership of the original. You can grant the client a license to use the original for a prescribed time, after which possession shall be returned to you.

Both New York and California have statutes that protect the artist's reproduction rights and ownership of the original artwork, but these statutes differ slightly. California provides that the artist reserves all reproduction rights not expressly granted in a signed agreement, but it limits this protection to works of fine art, as discussed earlier. Work prepared under a contract for advertising or trade use is not protected by this law.

Conversely, California reserves the creator's ownership of the original physical work in the case of a work of art, which is broadly defined as "any work of visual or graphic art of any media including, but not limited to, a painting, drawing, sculpture, craft, photograph or film."

New York's statute protects the creator's reproduction rights and ownership of the original work in the case of the more broad-

ly defined work of art. The states of Oregon and Oklahoma also have enacted legislation to protect the artist's reproduction rights.

The Copyright Act also provides some protection. Sections 201(d) and 204 state that a copyright, or any of the exclusive rights comprised in a copyright, may be transferred only by a written conveyance signed by the owner or her agent. (This provision does not apply to ownership of the original work of art, however.)

The safest way to ensure that the proper rights are reserved is to include express language in the contract between the artist and client explaining exactly which rights are being transferred, and that all other rights are reserved, as is ownership of all original artwork, if applicable. Language creating such reservations can be stated as follows:

This Agreement grants one-time [exclusive or nonexclusive] use of _____[project name]_____ for purposes of _____ for a period of _____ months/years. Any and all other rights and uses are reserved by the Artist, and transfer must be separately negotiated and invoiced, in writing.

[Optional] In the event Company desires to purchase all the rights to the project, Company shall pay a sale price of $_____.

Unless otherwise agreed in writing, all artwork prepared for _____[project name]_____ will be returned to Artist within _____ days of its submission, and ownership of same is retained and reserved by Artist.

In any contract, even where the client ends up owning all the rights through a buy-out or, as explained later, in a work made for hire, you should retain the right to reproduce your artwork for purposes of exhibitions, compilations, promotional portfolios, and other noncompeting personal uses. No client should object to this arrangement, as it has no effect on the rights transferred by the artist. If the client does object, he may be afraid that you will somehow use these reserved rights to compete with him. You must convince the client that you have no intent to compete and that these reserved rights are too limited to permit any competitive uses.

Finally, if the client wants additional rights but is unwilling to pay for them, a royalty arrangement may be agreeable. In this way, you'll receive a percentage of the client's profits from sales of reproductions of your work. These payments should be made when profits accrue to the client, and they should be accompanied by regular accountings showing how the royalty was calculated for each pay period, usually quarterly or semiannually. The client may go along with this arrangement because she will have to pay a royalty only when she realizes a profit. The point is, don't give away something for nothing. Get paid for the labor of creating a work of art, and get paid for each use of that work.

Work Made For Hire

You should avoid having your work characterized as a *"work made for hire."* A work made for hire is the property of the client, or employer, as soon as it is created. You as the artist would have no rights in the work, because the client is considered the creator, or author, in the eyes of the law. Let's take a look at what that means.

The rights granted to a creator of an original work by the Copyright Act of 1976 include the reproduction of the work in copies in or on any kind of article, useful or otherwise; the distribution of copies by sale, rental, lease, or other transfer of ownership; the preparation of a new work based on the original work; and the public display of the work.

The owner of a copyrighted work has certain remedies to prevent others infringing those rights. The copyright owner can stop the infringer from continuing the infringing activities; the infringing copies can be impounded and destroyed or disposed of; the owner can seek damages and profits from

the infringer, as well as the cost of suing the infringer and attorney's fees; and the infringer may be subject to criminal penalties.

All of these rights and remedies belong to the owner of the copyright. If you create a work made for hire, they belong not to you, but to your client or employer.

Your work can be classified as a work made for hire in one of two ways. If you are an employee and your artwork is prepared for your employer as part of your job, the artwork will be work made for hire. Your employer becomes the author of the work as soon as it is created and is the original owner of the copyright. You are simply the employed artist with no rights at all, other than those granted by your employment contract.

If you do not create the artwork within the scope of your employment, you generally retain ownership of the copyright. Say, for example, you work as a grocery store clerk, and you have an idea for some artwork and your employer wants to use your work as a promotional or advertising gimmick. The artwork would not be within the normal course of your job, and without an agreement to the contrary, would not be a work made for hire. The problem is that in less clear-cut cases, a court may find that your artwork was created within the scope of your employment, even though you felt that it wasn't.

You can attempt to have your employment contract written so that any artwork you create cannot be considered work made for hire. In that case your employment agreement should state:

No work created by _____(artist)_____ for _____(client)_____ whether created within or outside the scope of _____(artist's)_____ employment, shall be considered a "work made for hire" as defined by sections 101 and 201(b) of the Copyright Act of 1976.

The other way for you to end up in a work-made-for-hire situation is if you are specially ordered or commissioned to create a work that fits one of several categories, and there is a written agreement signed by all parties involved, that the work will be considered a work made for hire. The categories include:

- Contribution to a collective work, such as a magazine, anthology, or encyclopedia
- Contribution to a motion picture or other audiovisual work
- Supplementary work, which is a work prepared to supplement that of another author, for various purposes such as illustration, explanation, or comment, as when you provide some illustrations for a novel written by someone else
- An instructional text prepared for use in systematic instructional activities

In all nonemployment situations, you should sign a contract before any artwork is submitted to a client or before you agree to prepare a commissioned work, and the pertinent language should read as follows:

No work prepared by ____(artist)____ for ____(client)____, pursuant to this agreement or any other agreement, shall be considered a "work made for hire" as defined by sections 101 and 201(b) of the Copyright Act of 1976.

When you create a work made for hire, you have no rights other than those created by a written and signed agreement. You have no reproduction rights or other residual rights. You are not entitled to stop others from infringing on the copyright in your work. Even the state legislation discussed in the previous sections of this chapter generally does not apply to the artist who creates works made for hire.

It is quite obvious that it is not in your best interest to have your work considered a work made for hire. The best way to avoid it is by a written and signed contract executed before your artwork is prepared, whether or not you are an employee.

The Fine Prints Disclosure Law

Some states have enacted a law that requires dealers in *fine prints* to disclose certain information to buyers of those prints, such as the name of the artist; whether the artist signed the print and how many were signed; the medium and manner of reproductions; how the master was used; and how many prints were produced if the edition was limited.

Fine prints may be defined as engravings, etchings, woodcuts, serigraphs, silk screens, photographs, or similar art objects, depending on which state is involved.

The states that currently require fine prints disclosure are Arkansas, California, Florida, Georgia, Hawaii, Illinois, Maryland, Minnesota, New York, Oregon, and South Carolina.

As a penalty for providing false information, the seller of a fine print must refund the purchase price. The buyer may also be entitled to three times the purchase price if the seller knowingly defrauded them.

Fine print disclosure laws are obviously intended as consumer protection, but these laws do protect your career as well, because they discourage the production and distribution of unauthorized copies of your work. Also, if you sell directly to the public, you may be subject to these laws and penalties, if you provide false information.

Unfair Competition and Trademarks

A *trademark* is a symbol, logo, phrase, or a combination of all three placed on a product or used in conjunction with a service provided to the buying public. The mark is used to identify a company or manufacturer, and it distinguishes that company's products from those of its competitors.

Trademarks registered in the Federal Patent and Trademark Office are accorded protection under the Lanham Act, which prevents a diversion of sales through a competitor's use of the owner's mark or of one that is confusingly similar. The owner's reputation is also protected from damage when the competitor's product is of inferior quality and the public might confuse the inferior product with that of the mark's owner. State trademark laws provide similar protection.

Trademark law can help you as an artist by protecting your use of your name or a distinctive logo. It may prevent misappropriation of your name, or under certain circumstances, your work.

Trademark law can be seen as a specific category of unfair competition law. Unfair competition exists when there is confusion as to the origin of products or services, because of the passing off of one's goods as those of another, or the appropriation of the good will and reputation established by another's distinctive product name or appearance.

The elements of unfair competition are generally prescribed by state legislatures and common law established by state courts and, therefore, may differ. One state may require that an actual "palming off" must be proven, while another state simply may need proof that the competing product would create a likelihood of confusion as to the source of the products. The basic test, though, is whether persons exercising reasonable intelligence and discrimination would be taken in by the similarity.

Depending upon the circumstances, the law of unfair competition can provide you, as an artist, with a broad range of protection:

■ It can prevent your being presented as the author of a work you did not create, or a work that is an altered version of your own;

■ It can prevent others from taking credit for the creation of your work;

■ It can prevent others from using titles for their works that are identical or similar to those you have used for your works. It is generally necessary, in this instance, that your titles have acquired a "secondary meaning," in that the public identifies the use of those titles with your work.

■ As stated earlier, it will prevent others from unfairly competing with you by confusing the public and benefiting from the reputation you have established for your product's name, appearance, and style. Of course, if you give away your right to be credited with authorship of a work, the law of unfair competition isn't going to return that right to you.

Any action based on the theory of unfair competition generally must be brought in a state court, as state law establishes the concept. In addition, the federal Lanham Act, which is the law governing federally registered trademarks, provides that anyone who uses "a false designation of origin, or any false description or representation" in selling goods or services is liable in a civil action brought by anyone damaged or likely to be damaged by the false representation.

This statute is considered to be a codification of certain unfair competition remedies. It has not been widely used, but it may provide artists with a means to prevent unfair competition in federal court.

It should be understood that, when bringing a legal action against another for unfair competition, for infringement of a trademark or a copyright, or for a breach of contract, it is generally necessary to retain competent counsel. The intricacies of the theories of the law involved in such actions are generally too complex for laypersons, as well as for attorneys not specializing in the arts and entertainment field.

The various remedies available under the laws of contracts, copyright, trademark, and unfair competition are all subject to statutes of limitation. These statutes require that you file a legal action within a specified number of years after your rights have been infringed upon. The number of years varies from state to state and depends on what kind of right has been infringed. One example, though, is that under the Copyright Act of 1976, you must commence your civil action within three years after your claim accrued. After three years have passed, you will have no right to sue the infringer. If the infringement is ongoing, you will have the right to claim damages for any infringing actions that have taken place up to three years prior to the date you commenced suit.

You can also protect your rights in other ways. You can learn the best way to conduct your business for the protection of yourself and your clients. You should use written contracts, which must be signed by all parties involved. Each contract should clearly reflect what was agreed to by you and your client, and each person should get a copy with original signatures as evidence of the agreement. If it was agreed that you will get an artist's credit, then the contract should say that you will get it. If the project is not to be considered a work made for hire, this must be stated in writing, as should all terms that have been negotiated.

A recent study and survey published by the United States Copyright Office's Catalogue of Entries revealed that 71.8 percent of 206 visual artists polled never placed a copyright notice on their works. This inaction could give rise to a loss of copyright ownership, which once lost, can never be retrieved. If artists are reluctant to protect their own reputations and artworks under current laws, it is doubtful that new protective legislation will be effective. You must undertake the responsibility of learning how to conduct business as an artist, as such knowledge will benefit you, your business, and your clients.

COMMONLY ASKED QUESTIONS: MORAL RIGHTS

Q. *Is there any way around a work-for-hire contract? Is there any clause I can insert that will make it better?*

A. If you enter a contract that states it is a work-for-hire assignment, and it complies with the work-for-hire section of the Copyright Act, there's no way to avoid it. You cannot insert a clause to the contrary if it is a work-for-hire agreement. In a work-for-hire contract, you can make certain demands, however. You should ask for name credit and royalties. Even though you don't hold the copyright, you can still negotiate payments prior to signing the contract.

Q. *I've shied away from entering contests because they seem to buy all rights. Is this a customary practice?*

A. Avoid any contest that requires you to transfer all rights to your entries. Most contests ask to reserve the right to the ownership of the copies you send so that they can hold on to the entries. However, you can still own the copyright while the contest owns the illustration.

(*Editorial note:*) Also, make sure you understand the difference between a contest and an art competition. A contest usually involves a solution to a certain problem, such as letterhead design, while a competition generally restricts its entries by media and perhaps style, leaving the subject matter open. Contests can be a hidden form of work on speculation: sometimes an opportunistic sponsor is seeking a variety of solutions to his problem in a convenient, inexpensive way. Before you enter a contest, read the rules. You should be asked to submit only representative samples first, then supply sketches or comprehensives after being selected as a semifinalist. Also, if you're asked to submit roughs, you should receive a letter of agreement stating who owns the art, whether or not you will receive a credit line, and how much you will be paid.

Q. *Is a commission a work-for-hire agreement?*

A. It can be under certain conditions. It depends upon how your contract is drafted. If you were commissioned to illustrate a collective work such as a magazine, or contribute to an audiovisual work such as a film, or if you are illustrating instructional text or are supplementing text with illustrations, such as in a book, you are creating works made for hire if your contract reads that way. This covers a lot of markets that illustrators work in—book publishing and magazines. If you are commissioned to illustrate a magazine or book, protect yourself against work-for-hire by including this statement in your agreement:

> No work created by
> _____ for
> _____, whether
> created within or outside the scope of employment, shall be considered a "work-for-hire" as defined by sections 101 and 201(b) of the Copyright Act of 1976.

Q. *If I own the copyright to a work, don't I automatically have the right of paternity?*

A. Copyright gives you the exclusive right under federal law to reproduce, sell, distribute, display, and publish your work, and it protects you from infringement. It does *not*, however, provide that you must be given credit when your work is displayed or reproduced. The right of paternity gives you the right, which you can pursue in state court, to be credited with the authorship of fine art. It also gives you the right to disclaim authorship if your work is altered without permission, or if you were not the creator.

In states with paternity rights laws, the right of paternity usually covers original paintings, sculptures, and drawings; it excludes prints, photographs, and works of art created under a "contract for commercial use." Graphic artists may not be able to claim right of paternity on commissioned works. Therefore, it is important for illustrators and designers to make sure their contracts state that they receive name credit along with all copies of the work.

Q. *I was commissioned by a newspaper to illustrate a piece in the paper's Sunday supplement. I submitted the work, but the art director wanted several changes made. He said he didn't have time to return it to me for the alterations and would touch it up himself. I agreed. When it was printed, it was a mess. I was ashamed to have my name attached to it. At least I got paid. But what can I do about my artwork—and maybe my reputation—being ruined?*

A. You verbally agreed to the alteration, so you are bound to your agreement. In the future, request in a written contract that only you make necessary alterations. This is a contractual matter; the rights of paternity and integrity do not apply to commercial works under state moral rights laws.

EASY REFERENCE CHECKLISTS: MORAL RIGHTS

Moral rights fall into three categories:
- [ ] Right of creation protects your right to control publication of your work
- [ ] Right of paternity is the right to claim or disclaim authorship
- [ ] Right of integrity is the right to modify your work or prevent its mutilation, distortion, or alteration

States with moral rights laws:
- [ ] California
- [ ] Louisiana
- [ ] Maine
- [ ] Massachusetts
- [ ] New Jersey
- [ ] New York
- [ ] Pennsylvania
- [ ] Rhode Island

Red flags to avoid in agreements:
- [ ] Work on speculation
- [ ] Buy-outs, or selling all rights
- [ ] Transfer of ownership of original art
- [ ] Work made for hire
- [ ] Unbillable changes

CHAPTER 3
CONTRACTS

By Jean S. Perwin

Many artists view contracts as scary and complicated things. They don't have to be. In this chapter, we will look at what contracts are and how to use them.

The chapter deals primarily with the contracts you will need as a fine artist or graphic artist. I will not be discussing other types of contracts, such as leases or divorce settlements or contracts to buy furniture or to go on a group tour to Athens. While the general contract principles apply to every kind of contract, the discussion here is limited to contracts affecting your work as an artist.

WHAT IS A CONTRACT?

A contract is a fairly simple thing. It is a promise for which the law gives you a remedy if it's broken. Or, put another way, it is a promise attached to an obligation. The following example illustrates the difference between a promise and a legally binding contract.

Suppose you invite a friend to dinner and ask him to bring his guitar. "I promise," he says. If he forgets the guitar, you may still feed him, but you have not created a legal contract.

If, though, you are having a fancy dinner party and say to the same friend, "I'll pay you one hundred fifty dollars to play the guitar at my party," and he agrees, you have created a contract.

Why? Because the law says a promise

must have certain elements to be considered a contract. The first of those elements is *parties*—in this case, you and your friend. The second is *consent*. The first example contains no legal consent, because the parties have not attached enough significance to the agreement. In the second example, legal consent is probably present because of the offer of money, which is the next element—*consideration*. In many contracts, the critical element that makes it legally binding is an exchange of consideration or, in most cases, money. In the first example, there is no consideration given in exchange for the promise. In the second, there is. Finally, a contract requires that an *obligation* be created. In the first example, there is none created. In the second, there is. So when all of these elements are present in a transaction and you have the ability to invoke the law, you have a legally binding agreement.

In the art business, promises usually take the form of agreements to do some kind of artwork in exchange for money. Whether oral or written, these promises are contracts.

THE ADVANTAGE OF CONTRACTS

Disputes generally arise because the parties have differing conceptions of what the agreement said or meant. Words very often have a different meaning to the speaker and the hearer. The reason that contracts are important to you is that they force you and the person you are contracting with—be it a magazine, a gallery, or an ad agency—to be clear about what you both mean. They prevent the hearer and the speaker from attaching different meanings to the same words. They are business tools. That's all. Once you get used to using them, they are not so scary. In fact, they can be invaluable when a disagreement arises. Often a contract or something in writing can be the dif-

Jean S. Perwin is a Miami, Florida-based attorney specializing in intellectual property law. She represents artists, art galleries, and many art-related businesses in copyrights, contract, and corporate matters. She has contributed articles to The Artist's Magazine *and has served as counsel to government agencies. She received her J.D. degree from the Boston College Law School.*

ference between a lot of money and none at all.

WHEN DO YOU NEED A CONTRACT?

This section could more appropriately be called, When do you need something in writing? The answer is, always. Samuel Goldwyn is credited with having first said that an oral contract is not worth the paper it's written on. Mr. Goldwyn knew whereof he spoke. While oral contracts are legally enforceable, they are very difficult to enforce.

You should have a contract for any commission or job. Even if you're not getting paid, you can receive name credit and a copyright notice. However, you should insist on signing a contract for jobs that pay more than $100. Every little bit helps, but anything less than $100 wouldn't be worth the legal fees to fight for it.

You especially need a contract when you enter a long-term business relationship. If someone is going to publish your work, display it, sell it for you, or reproduce it for you in multiple copies, you will be involved in a relationship that will extend over time. Circumstances change, and when they do, problems arise. A contract can prevent little problems from becoming big, expensive ones. That is not to say you necessarily need a long, multipage document filled with *whereofs* and *hereinafters*. What it means is that you should have something in writing that outlines the terms of your agreement. It can be as simple as a receipt for a sale or a short letter. It does not have to be a traditionally worded legal contract.

How to Get Everything in Writing

Very often, beginning artists are afraid that if they insist on a contract they will somehow sour the deal. You won't. But if you are nervous about it, here are some suggestions of other ways to get things in writing.

One way to present the idea of a contract to a prospective employer or purchaser is to present it as something you always do as a way to keep track of your commitments, for example, "This is a standard form contract I keep in my file so I have a record of all the

work I'm doing."

A second way to have something in writing is to make sure that your proposals, forms, or stationery have the appropriate protective language printed in them. (See the example on page 62.) This is the simplest way to protect yourself without having to write an actual contract.

Letters are invaluable, nonthreatening ways to reduce the terms of your agreement to writing. Here is a simple, three-sentence letter that can be used in many situations.

(Date)

Dear. . . . :

It was a pleasure speaking with you on (date) about turning my (drawing, painting, etc.) into posters. It is my understanding that I will supply you with (specifications) and that you will pay me ($), payable half now and half on final delivery of (specifications).

I look forward to working with you.

Sincerely,

WHEN DO YOU NEED A LAWYER?

Despite our dreadful reputations, lawyers can be extremely helpful people. The forms in this book can help you draft an adequate contract without a lawyer if your circumstances fit the form. But if you face a situation that is unique or complicated, if you are negotiating for a large sum of money, or if just looking at the contract gives you a headache, it's a good idea to see a lawyer.

If you are presented with a contract drawn up by someone else, it's helpful to have an attorney review it. I had an artist-client who signed a contract with a publisher without having it reviewed. It did not contain a kill fee. The publisher decided two years later not to publish the book, and the artist was out a lot of time and money and had no book to show for it. A lawyer would have prevented this loss. Remember that any contract with a large organization is drafted to protect the organization, and not you. While you may not be in a position to demand a lot of money, an attorney can advise you about exactly what terms you're agreeing to and help you to negotiate more favorable terms.

Most lawyers will work with you on fees. Fees vary, so shop around. Try to find an attorney who is familiar with the art business. Ask friends for recommendations. If there's a Volunteer Lawyers for the Arts program in your city, they can recommend sympathetic lawyers. It's far cheaper to pay an attorney to help you with a contract at the beginning than it is to pay one after things have gone wrong. Think of it as an investment in your career. The same lawyer can help you at many other points as well. She can file a copyright application, incorporate your business, register a trademark, and provide you with information on art-related statutes, such as fine print statutes and consignment laws.

EVALUATING A CONTRACT: RED FLAGS

Before you consult a lawyer, you should look for contract terms that should be red flags to any artist.

Manner of Payment: Do not sign a contract that does not specify how you get paid. Any contract should have not only the amount you will be paid, but also a description of how and when. For example, the contract should specify payment within ten days after final delivery; or half now, the balance on delivery; or installments of a certain amount each month.

Copyright Rights: If you are presented with a contract that says "work for hire" or "all rights purchased," look at it very carefully. If you sign a contract that contains these terms, the work created under the contract becomes the property of the other party. They will be able to use it in any way they wish without paying you, consulting you, or, depending on the terms of the contract, crediting you. Consult Chapter 1 for a detailed explanation of these terms. Make sure you understand them.

Always try to keep your copyright rights. Any contract on any work that will be published should specify that a copyright notice will be included in the published work.

Reproduction Rights: Make sure that any contract you sign reserves all your other reproduction rights. The right to reproduce your work is one of the most valuable you have. Look carefully at what rights you are selling, and get paid for each type of reproduction right.

Although retaining ownership of the copyright gives you the legal right to prevent someone from making reproductions of your work, the contract should spell out clearly what is being bought and sold. Specifically reserving reproduction rights is added protection. For example, if you are creating a poster for an art festival, your effort to share in the profits from the beach towel they decide to make from the poster will be greatly enhanced by your reservation of reproduction rights in your contract.

Termination and Cancellation: Very often, contracts will provide for termination by the other party but not by you. The contract should provide for termination by both parties. If the contract asks you to do a lot of work on speculation before getting paid, be sure there is some kind of cancellation or *kill* fee, so that if the contract is canceled, you are compensated for the work you have done.

Artistic Control: This varies in every contract. But watch out for any language that gives the other party total control of what you're doing. For example, don't allow the buyer to make changes in the work or design without consulting with you. In this area, even novices can exercise some negotiating strength. People who hire designers or artists will often be willing to allow them control over the artistic decisions required in producing the work. If you are allowing prints to be made from your work, for example, the more say you have over the process, the better you can guarantee that the final product will be to your satisfaction.

Insurance and Delivery Costs: This has been a contentious item in many contracts I have seen. The costs of packing, transporting, and insuring a large work can be very great. Make sure you determine in advance who is to pay these costs and any other expenses that may arise.

Independent Contractor Status: If you are working freelance and have more than one agreement in effect at a time, you may want to make clear that you are an independent contractor and not an employee. The difference is that very significant legal obligations attach to the employer/employee relationship having to do with the amount of control exercised over you and the work.

Expenses: Make sure the contract is clear about who pays them and how they are to be paid, including when or whether receipts are necessary.

Time is of the Essence: This innocent-sounding phrase has serious legal consequences. It means that the failure to meet obligations stated in the contract on time will constitute a material breach of the contract. For example, if you promise to complete a drawing in two weeks and you do it in four weeks and the contract you signed states that time is of the essence, the fact that you were late will be very significant if there is a lawsuit based on the contract.

TECHNICALITIES

In the course of negotiating a contract, some things may affect the contract, but are not specifically stated in it. These things don't come up very often, but they exist and should be noted.

The Uniform Commercial Code: The UCC is a statute adopted by every state but Louisiana that governs the sale of goods. Art is considered "goods" under the UCC if its value is over $500. If there is a dispute over the sale of finished artwork or a commissioned piece priced at $500 or more, the UCC controls the types of remedies that are available to you. The code does not apply if you are supplying services to someone.

The UCC establishes these restrictions:

Competency: If either you or the person you are contracting with is insane or under legal age (twenty-one or eighteen in most states), your contract will be unenforceable.

Purpose: You cannot contract for a purpose that is illegal or against public policy. So contracts to forge artwork or smuggle art would not be enforceable.

Warranties: Warranties are guarantees the law attaches to certain situations to protect one or both of the parties. They are assumptions made about the sale, and if they prove false, the law provides you a remedy. The UCC specifies these warranties in the sale of goods:

1. That the artist owns the work he's selling.
2. That the work will be fit for the purpose for which it is sold.
3. That the work is unique.

If any of these assumptions are untrue, the contract is voidable.

Statute of Limitations: The Statute of Limitations limits the time you have to sue someone after he has breached a contract. For sale of goods under the UCC, it is four years. For other contracts, it varies from state to state. If you think you have a legal claim against someone, don't wait.

SPECIFIC CONTRACTS

What follows are samples of contracts that have been used successfully by many artists. They afford basic legal protection for most art or design-related transactions. However, they are only forms. They must always be tailored to your circumstances. They do not constitute legal advice. They should be used to give you ideas of things to consider when discussing the sale or use of your work.

In using these forms, remember their terms are negotiable. They are drafted for the protection of the artist, but if you are uncomfortable with any particular provision or your prospective employer is hesitant about anything, their terms can be changed. The only things I would not recommend eliminating are the points covered in the section "Evaluating a Contract: Red Flags." You can also use these contracts to assemble a new one, using clauses from different places that reflect your own needs more accurately.

To make these contracts easier to use, I have divided them by career stages. There are contracts for the beginning stages of a career, more complicated contracts for the middle stages, contracts for the more established artist in the later stages, and some miscellaneous contracts that may prove useful at any point.

EARLY-STAGE CONTRACTS

When you first sell your work, you are often not terribly concerned with the legal implications of that sale. You're just happy that someone will actually pay you for your work. The contracts in this section are essentially bills of sale. They are writings to accompany the sale of work—whether it's the sale of something you've already created or the sale of something someone has asked you to create (a commissioned piece). Think of them as receipts. They record the transaction.

Never sell anything without using one of these forms.

For artists, early-stage contracts serve several important functions. The first and the most important is the reservation of reproduction rights. On the front of the bill of sale, it's clearly stated that your rights are reserved. On the invoice and purchase order, the terms clearly state what rights are transferred by payment of the invoice. One of the most common legal problems during the early stage of an artist's career is future reproductive use. For example, you might sell an illustration to a magazine for one use and find it reproduced in another magazine a year later. That is why it is so important to use an invoice form that contains protective terms in it. Another important aspect is that these forms provide a record of sales. That record is important for developing mailing lists, for tax purposes, and for future contracts.

This section includes a simple bill of sale, two purchase orders and a general all-purpose form that can be used to make estimates, confirm work, or invoice completed work.

BILL OF SALE:

Use this simple receipt form when you sell work to a gallery, to a collector, to a purchaser at an art show, to an interior decorator, to a friend to give as a wedding present—to anyone where the sale is the end of the transaction. The purchaser wants to own it. Period. This form is the absolute minimum you need to protect yourself in the event of the unforeseen.

Bill of Sale

Place: _____
(Business, gallery, art show or studio address)

Sold to: _____
(Name)

_____
(Address)

Description of
Work: _____

_____

Price:
Terms of _____
Payment: _____

REPRODUCTION RIGHTS RESERVED

_____
(Purchaser)

_____
(Artist or authorized dealer)

Date: _____

ESTIMATE/CONFIRMATION/INVOICE:

This contract is an excellent all-purpose form for beginning artists to use. It can be printed on your letterhead and adapted to almost any situation. The terms cover almost all of the problems encountered by beginning illustrators and designers—how you get paid, who pays expenses, cancellation fees, and copyright ownership. It provides space for you to include all relevant information. When you are starting out, have this form printed on your letterhead and use it for everything. You will have sound, basic legal coverage if anything should go wrong. Don't forget to keep copies.

Estimate/Confirmation/Invoice

(Your Letterhead)

_____ Estimate   _____ Invoice # _____   _____ Assignment Confirmation

To: Date:

Description of Assignment

Delivery Date _____
(Predicated on receipt of all materials to be supplied by client)

Total Fee _____

EXPENSES:

These expense amounts are _____ Estimates

_____ Final

Client shall reimburse designer for all expenses

Illustration Photography   _____

Materials and Supplies   _____

Mechanicals   _____

Messengers   _____

Photographic Reproduction   _____

Printing   _____

Toll Telephones   _____

Transportation and Travel   _____

Models and Props   _____

Shipping and Insurance   _____

Type   _____

Stats   _____

Other   _____

Subtotal _____

Sales Tax _____

Total Due _____

Any usage rights not exclusively transferred are reserved to designer. Usage beyond that granted to client herein shall require payment of a mutually agreed upon additional fee subject to all terms on reverse.

Rights transferred. Designer transfers to the client the following exclusive rights of usage:

Title or Product	_____
Category of Use	_____
Medium of Use	_____
Edition (if book)	_____
Geographic Area	_____
Time Period	_____

Any usage rights not exclusively transferred are reserved to designer. Usage beyond that granted to client herein shall require payment of a mutually agreed upon additional fee subject to all terms.

TERMS:

1. TIME FOR PAYMENT. All invoices are payable within thirty (30) days of receipt. A 1½% monthly service charge is payable on all overdue balances. The grant of any license or right of copyright is conditioned on receipt of full payment.

2. ESTIMATES. If this form is used for an estimate or assignment confirmation, the fees and expenses shown are minimum estimates only. Final fees and expenses shall be shown when invoice is rendered. Client's approval shall be obtained for any increases in fees or expenses that exceed the original estimate by 10% or more.

3. CHANGES. Client shall be responsible for making additional payments for changes requested by Client in original assignment. However, no additional payment shall be made for changes required to conform to the original assignment description. The Client shall offer the Designer the first opportunity to make any changes.

4. EXPENSES. Client shall reimburse Designer for all expenses arising from this assignment, including the payment of any sales taxes due on this assignment, and shall advance $_____ to the Designer for payment of said expenses.

5. CANCELLATION. In the event of cancellation of this assignment, ownership of all copyrights and the original artwork is retained by the Designer and a cancellation fee for work completed, based on the contract price and expenses already incurred, shall be paid by the Client.

6. OWNERSHIP OF ARTWORK. The Designer retains ownership of all original artwork, whether preliminary or final, and the Client shall return such artwork within thirty (30) days of use.

7. CREDIT LINES. The Designer and any other creators shall receive a credit line with any editorial usage. If similar credit lines are to be given with other types of usage, it must be so indicated here.

_____

_____

8. RELEASES. Client will indemnify Designer against all claims and expenses, including reasonable attorney's fees, due to uses for which no release was requested in writing or for uses which exceed authority granted by a release.

9. MODIFICATIONS. Modification of the agreement must be written, except that the invoice may include, and Client shall be obligated to pay, fees or expenses that were orally authorized in order to progress promptly with work.

10. ACCEPTANCE OF TERMS. The above terms incorporate Article 2 of the Uniform Commercial Code. If not objected to within ten (10) days, these terms shall be deemed acceptable.

_____
Your Signature

_____
Company Name

_____
Authorized Signature

_____
Name and Title

_____
Date

PURCHASE ORDERS:

When you start out in the graphic design business, you often sell one thing at a time. The bill of sale can be used in any sales situation, but here are two samples of simple purchase orders that are more specific to graphic artists.

The first one is a very simple form for the purchase of an illustration to be used for one purpose. The contract here is for a book jacket. It may be altered for a magazine cover, a brochure design, or any one-shot design assignment. It spells out in detail exactly what the job requires, as well as what reproduction rights are being purchased by the publisher and which are reserved to the artist.

The second one is more detailed and has more legal protection in it. For example, it is more specific about the time for payment and expenses. It addresses what happens if the contract is cancelled and specifically discusses what happens if the work turns up somewhere else without your authorization (Section 7). As a general rule, it is better to have more than you need in a contract. When in doubt, use Purchase Order #2.

Purchase Order #1

(Your Letterhead)

PUBLISHER _____

ADDRESS _____

BOOK TITLE _____ AUTHOR _____

Edition: Hardcover _____ Paperback _____ Other _____

Fee _____

Trim Size _____

Number of Colors _____

Description of Job _____

The publisher owns exclusive reproduction rights to the total jacket design with art and/or photography for packaging, advertising, publicity, or any other means of promotion for the edition described above. Any change or alteration in the total design or illustration must be with artist's consent and approval.

The artist retains all other rights to the artwork. Any further uses of the artwork (book club edition, film version, paperback edition, foreign edition) will be negotiated in a separate agreement at the discretion of the artist.

The artist will not reproduce, give or sell reproduction rights of said artwork for any purpose unrelated to the original book.

The publisher agrees to have © appear on the flap of the jacket with the year and the artist's name. The artist guarantees that copyright does not infringe on any other.

The publisher will return all artwork (illustration, photography) to the artist in thirty (30) days after production of the jacket is completed.

SIGNED FOR THE PUBLISHER _____

SIGNED FOR ARTIST _____

DATE _____

Purchase Order #2

TO _____ DATE _____

_____

DESCRIPTION OF ASSIGNMENT _____

_____

_____

_____

DELIVERY DATE _____ FEE _____

BUYER SHALL REIMBURSE ARTIST FOR THE FOLLOWING EXPENSES:

_____

_____

_____

_____

_____

THE BUYER PURCHASES THE FOLLOWING EXCLUSIVE RIGHTS OF USAGE:

Title or Product _____

Category of Use_____

Medium of Use_____

Edition (of book)_____

Geographic Area_____

Time Period_____

Artist reserves any usage rights not expressly transferred. Any usage beyond that granted to buyer herein shall require the payment of a mutually agreed upon additional fee, subject to all terms below.

TERMS:

1. TIME FOR PAYMENT. All invoices shall be paid within thirty (30) days of receipt.

2. CHANGES. Buyer shall make additional payments for changes requested in original assignment. However, no additional payment shall be made for changes required to conform to the original assignment description. The Buyer shall offer the Artist first opportunity to make any changes.

3. EXPENSES. Buyer shall reimburse Artist for all expenses arising from this assignment, including but not limited to all those listed above, and the payment of any sales taxes due on this assignment. Buyer's approval shall be obtained for any increases in fees or expenses that exceed the original estimate by 10% or more.

4. CANCELLATION. In the event of cancellation of this assignment, ownership of all copyrights and the original artwork shall be retained by the Artist, and a cancellation fee for work completed, based on the contract price and expenses already incurred, shall be paid by the Buyer.

5. OWNERSHIP OF ARTWORK. The Artist retains ownership of all original artwork, whether preliminary or final, and the Buyer shall return such artwork within thirty (30) days of use.

6. CREDIT LINES. Credit line shall be in the form:

© _____ 19 _____

The Buyer shall give Artist and any other creators a credit line with any editorial usage.

7. RELEASES. Buyer shall indemnify Artist against all claims and expenses, including reasonable attorney's fees, due to uses for which no release was requested in writing or for uses which exceed authority granted by a release.

8. MODIFICATIONS. Modification of the Agreement must be written, except that the invoice may include, and Buyer shall pay, fees or expenses that were orally authorized in order to progress promptly with the work.

_____
ARTIST'S SIGNATURE

_____
COMPANY NAME

_____
AUTHORIZED SIGNATURE

_____
NAME AND TITLE

MIDDLE-STAGE CONTRACTS

This group of contracts represents the next stage of an artist's career. You have sold your artwork and are developing ongoing relationships with publishers or other buyers. You are busier. The projects are getting bigger. At this point, you might need many different contracts. They include a more detailed sales contract, gallery consignment agreement, print reproduction contract, licensing agreement, and magazine purchase order.

SALES CONTRACT:

This sales contract is also called an Agreement of Original Transfer of Artwork. Use it when you want to retain some control over the work after it leaves your hands. For example, the contract provides that you will be notified of exhibitions and requires that, if anything happens to the work, you will be the one to restore it. It also reserves reproduction rights. If you are selling a drawing and you don't care what happens to it, use the simple sales form in the previous section. If you do care how it's used or displayed, use a variation of this contract.

Agreement of Original Transfer of Artwork

Artist: _____   Address: _____

Purchaser: _____   Address: _____

WHEREAS Artist has created that certain work of art ("the Work"):

Title: _____

Dimensions: _____

Media: _____

Year: _____

WHEREAS the parties want the Artist to have certain rights in the future economics and integrity of the Work. The parties mutually agree as follows:

1. SALE: Artist hereby sells the Work to Purchaser at the agreed value of $_____

2. NOTICE OF EXHIBITION: Before committing the Work to a show, Purchaser must give Artist notice of intent to do so, telling Artist all the details of the show that Purchaser then knows.

3. PROVENANCE: Upon request, Artist will furnish Purchaser and his successors a written history and provenance of the Work, based on the Artist's best information as to shows.

4. ARTIST EXHIBITION: Artist may show the Work for up to 60 days once every five years at a non-profit institution at no expense to Purchaser, upon written notice no later than 120 days before opening and upon satisfactory proof of insurance and prepaid transportation.

5. NON-DESTRUCTION: Purchaser will not permit any intentional destruction, damage or modification of the Work.

6. RESTORATION: If the Work is damaged, Purchaser will consult Artist before any restoration and must give Artist first opportunity to restore it, if practicable.

7. RENTS: If the Work is rented, Purchaser must pay Artist 50 percent of the rent within 30 days of receipt.

8. REPRODUCTION: Artist reserves all copyright rights and rights to reproduce the Work.

9. NOTICE: A notice, in the form below, must be permanently affixed to the Work, warning that ownership, etc., are subject to this contract. If, however, a document represents the Work or is part of the Work, the Notice must instead be a permanent part of that document.

NOTICE: Ownership, transfer, exhibition and reproduction of this Work of Art are subject to a certain Contract dated ＿＿＿＿＿ between:

Artist: ＿＿＿＿＿＿＿＿＿＿＿＿＿＿＿   Address: ＿＿＿＿＿＿＿＿＿＿＿＿＿

Purchaser: ＿＿＿＿＿＿＿＿＿＿＿＿＿   Address: ＿＿＿＿＿＿＿＿＿＿＿＿＿
Artist has a copy

10. EXPIRATION: This contract binds the parties, their heirs and all their successors in interest, and all Purchaser's obligations are attached to the Work and go with ownership of the Work, all for the life of the Artist and Artist's surviving spouse plus 21 years, except the obligation of Paragraphs 2, 3 and 4 shall last only for Artist's lifetime.

11. ATTORNEY'S FEES: In any proceeding to enforce any part of this contract, the aggrieved party shall be entitled to reasonable attorney's fees in addition to any available remedy.

_____
Date

_____
(Artist)

_____
(Purchaser)

Reprinted by permission of *The Artist's Magazine.*

CONSIGNMENT CONTRACTS:

Consignment agreements are generally made with art galleries that agree to sell your work in exchange for a percentage of the selling price. However, they may also be used with a store or hotel lobby—any situation in which you give someone your work to sell but you don't get paid until the sale is made. Do not give anyone your work to sell in a retail situation without a consignment agreement.

Here are examples of two types of consignment agreements. The first is a general agreement that you make with a gallery to sell any and all of your work. It is usually an exclusive agreement, which means that only that gallery can sell your work for the duration of the contract. (This type of consignment agreement is similar to an artist's representative contract, in that the gallery is acting as your agent for the purpose of selling your work, but it is *not* a rep agreement.)

If you are considering signing a general consignment contract with a gallery, make sure that you are comfortable with the arrangement, because this contract assumes a fairly long-term relationship with wide parameters. The specific details of the arrangement are not spelled out. For example, the specific works of art to be consigned are not listed. The contract calls only for a minimum price to be set, not necessarily the retail selling price.

General Consignment Agreement

The following constitutes the entire agreement with respect to the sale by _____ Gallery of sculptures, drawings and graphics created by _____ Artist.

1. For a period of _____ years (or months) commencing on the date of this agreement, _____ Gallery shall have the exclusive right, in any part of the world, to offer for sale and to authorize others to offer for sale, all items of art works created and owned by Artist. Artist shall initially deliver each such item of his work to Gallery at such location as may be designated by Gallery.

2. For the period of _____ years, Gallery shall have the exclusive right to arrange, and to authorize others to arrange, for the publication and/or sale, in any part of the world, of books and catalogues containing illustrated reproductions of the artwork of Artist.

3. For the period of _____ years, Gallery shall arrange for exhibitions of Artist's works in the Cities of _____, _____ and such other places as the parties shall jointly determine. Gallery shall be responsible for all of the expenses of such exhibitions, including advertising and catalogue costs and insurance, and shall bear the entire cost of storing all items of Artist's work delivered to Gallery pursuant to this agreement.

4. The parties acknowledge that Artist has furnished to Gallery photographs of each item of Artist's works owned by Artist on the date of this agreement. The price at which Gallery shall offer each such item for sale shall not be less than the price set forth on the back of such photograph. The parties shall jointly determine the minimum sales price to be charged as to those artworks to be created by Artist during the term of this agreement. Minimum prices may be changed from time to time in such manner as shall jointly be determined by the parties.

5. As compensation for Gallery's services in effecting the sale of a particular work, Gallery shall be entitled to retain _____ percent of the balance of the gross proceeds of the particular sale, as and for Gallery's commission for having effected such sale, with the remaining _____ percent of such balance, to be paid to Artist on a monthly basis.

6. All copyright and further reproduction rights to the consigned works shall remain with the artist.

7. Full responsibility for any consigned work lost, stolen, or damaged while in Gallery's possession shall be on Gallery.

8. Consigned works will be held in trust for benefit of artist and will not be subject to claim by creditor of Gallery.

9. In any proceeding to enforce any part of this contract, the aggrieved party shall be entitled to reasonable attorney's fees in addition to any available remedy.

10. Either party may terminate this agreement on 30 days' notice.

11. This agreement shall be construed in accordance with the laws of the State of

_____.

Dated this _____ day of _____, 19_____.

(Signatures)

ARTIST-GALLERY CONSIGNMENT AGREEMENT:

The Artist-Gallery Consignment Agreement is a more limited type of consignment contract. Use a form of this agreement when you are not familiar with the gallery and want to try out the relationship for a limited period of time and with limited number of artworks.

The agreement contains all the standard protections for an artist in a consignment agreement—copyright, insurance, etc. It also makes clear that the gallery is not your agent for purposes other than the works listed in the agreement. As of this writing, fifteen states have laws affecting the consignment of art. If you live or do business in Arizona, Arkansas, California, Colorado, Connecticut, Florida, Maryland, Massachusetts, Michigan, Minnesota, New Mexico, New York, Oregon, Washington, or Wisconsin, you should make sure that your agreement contains all the legal requirements for your state.

One common problem in consignment arrangements that I've seen is getting paid on time. Both of these contracts provide for timely payments, but you may want to provide for late fees or interest on delayed payments by adding the following phrase to Section 5 of both contracts: "A late fee of 1 percent per month will be added to payment received after thirty (30) days."

Another common problem with consignment agreements is what happens if a gallery goes bankrupt. Unfortunately, this happens frequently. Both contracts contain provisions making it clear that neither your work nor your money is subject to the claims of creditors. However, the law in every state is different. If your state has a consignment statute, you will have more protection. If not, depending on the law, the contract may not be able to help. If you find yourself with work in a gallery that has folded, see a lawyer as soon as possible. The faster you are able to respond, the better luck you will have getting your work returned and getting any money to which you are still entitled.

Artist-Gallery Consignment Agreement

1. You confirm receipt of my consigned artworks, in perfect condition unless otherwise noted, as follows:

2.

Title	Medium	Dimensions	Retail Price	Gallery Commission
1.				
2.				
3.				
4.				
5.				

3. This agreement applies only to works consigned under this agreement and does not make you a general agent for any other works.

4. I reserve the copyright and all reproduction rights to these works. The gallery will not permit any of the artworks to be copied, photographed or reproduced without my written permission. All approved reproductions will carry my copyright notice: © 19____ _____. The gallery will print on each bill of sale: "The right to copy, photograph or reproduce the artwork(s) identified here is reserved by the Artist, _____."

5. Upon sale of the work(s), the retail price less your commission will be remitted to me within thirty (30) days after the sale. The title to these works remains with me until the works are sold and I am paid in full, at which time the title passes directly to the purchaser.

6. You will assume full responsibility for any consigned work lost, stolen or damaged while in your possession. Consigned works may not be removed from your premises for purposes of rental, installment sales or on approval with a potential purchaser without my permission. The specified retail prices may not be changed without my permission. I may withdraw my works on thirty (30) days written notice. You may return to me any of the consigned works on thirty (30) days written notice.

7. The consigned works will be held in trust for my benefit and will not be subject to claim by a creditor of the gallery. This agreement will terminate automatically upon my death, or if the gallery becomes bankrupt or insolvent. Either party may terminate this agreement by giving sixty (60) days notice in writing to the other party. Upon termination, all of my consigned artworks will be returned to me within thirty (30) days at your expense and all accounts settled.

8. In any proceeding to enforce any part of this contract, the aggrieved party shall be entitled to reasonable attorney's fees in addition to any available remedy.

Sincerely,

Consented and agreed to:

_____
Gallery Name

_____
Name and Title

Reprinted by permission of *The Artist's Magazine*.

REPRODUCTION AGREEMENTS:

In all the previous discussions of contracts, I have been warning you to reserve reproduction rights. Here is what you are reserving them for. The opportunity to reproduce work is what keeps graphic artists in business; it can be profitable for fine artists as well. These two agreements are a letter-type reproduction agreement and a full-fledged contract.

The first contract is a letter from a gallery to an artist regarding the publication of woodcuts. It can be changed as needed to be a letter from you to the gallery. The important things in it are the terms: which woodcuts are used, how many, copyright designation, how much money is advanced, how royalties are paid, how long the agreement runs. If you use this letter as the basis for your own letter, be sure to change the language to reflect your own situation.

Letter Contract with Gallery for Prints

Dear Artist:

This letter is to be the agreement between you and _____ Gallery regarding the publication of _____. The works selected are as follows: _____ _____. You will create _____ impressions of each _____ _____ which are to be signed and numbered accordingly by you. You may print ten (10) additional proofs for your personal use, and these are to be signed as artist's proofs. You will affix copyright notice in your name to all prints and all copyrights and rights of reproduction shall be retained by you upon sales to purchasers. You will provide _____ Gallery with certification of the cancellation of the blocks after completion of the printing.

_____ Gallery shall be solely responsible for and pay all costs of the printing.

_____ Gallery will prepare the title page, descriptive material, and justification page.

Nonrefundable advances of _____ shall be paid to you upon delivery of each _____ prints. The minimum selling price of each _____ shall be _____.

_____ Gallery will exercise best efforts to sell the _____ and shall receive 50 percent of all sales revenues as its commission. The balance due you, after subtraction of any advances paid to you, shall be remitted on the first day of each month along with an accounting showing the sale price and number of prints sold and the inventory of prints remaining. Title to all work shall remain in you and pass directly to purchasers.

_____ Gallery will insure all work for at least the minimum sale price and any insurance proceeds shall be equally divided.

The term of this agreement shall be one (1) year. After one (1) year, this agreement shall continue unless terminated upon either party giving sixty (60) days written notice of termination to the other party. Upon termination the inventory remaining shall be equally divided between _____ Gallery and you. Your share shall be promptly delivered to you by _____ Gallery. If, however, termination is based upon a breach or default by _____ Gallery under this agreement, all inventory remaining shall be promptly delivered to you. You agree to sign such papers as may be necessary to effectuate this agreement.

Kindly return one copy of this letter with your signature below.

Sincerely,

President

CONSENTED AND AGREED TO:

_____
Artist

CONTRACT FOR REPRODUCTION OF ARTWORK:

The next contract is an excellent comprehensive contract for the reproduction of works of art. It includes every type of provision for the protection of the artist entering into a reproduction agreement. It provides for a payment schedule that may change after the first year, and it requires payment within thirty days after delivery (Section 2). It provides for copyright registration and copyright protection for the artist. More important, it makes clear that you are the owner of the work and any other derivative work resulting from the original art (Section 3).

This contract allows the purchaser, or the *reproducer*, to accept or reject the artwork, but it makes clear that you own it and have the ability to sell it elsewhere (Section 7). The purchaser also has the right of first refusal for any other works created by the artist (Section 9). Make sure that if you use this contract, you want to allow the purchaser that right.

Whenever you allow your work to be reproduced, make sure that you are credited *and* that the copyright notice symbol, ©, appears with it, as provided in Section 11 of this contract. Never let your work be reproduced without a copyright notice.

Agreement for Reproduction of Work of Art

THIS AGREEMENT, is made on the _____ day of _____, 19_____, by and between _____, ("Artist"), of _____,

_____, and _____, ("Second Party"), of

_____, _____.

WHEREAS, Artist desires to create new and original Works of Art and to have them reproduced for sale as prints, reproductions, posters or replicas, and

WHEREAS, Second Party is in the business of buying, reproducing, exhibiting, selling, publishing and publicly distributing Works of Art.

NOW, THEREFORE, in consideration of the premises, the considerations mentioned, and the mutual promises made, the parties agree as follows:

1. Second Party agrees to pay Artist for the rights to reproduce, sell and distribute Artist's work, and to reproduce, publish, exhibit, sell and distribute reproductions of Artists' work on the terms of this Agreement, and Artist agrees to create the following described Works of Art for reproductions:

Editions will be of _____ number, signed and numbered 1-_____. Artist agrees to supply Second Party with _____ additional copies signed for them and Artist shall retain for Artist's own use _____ copies designated as Artist's proofs.

2. The parties agree that the price per edition for the first year will be _____ ($_____) Dollars; the second year _____ ($_____) Dollars; the third year _____ ($_____) Dollars. Payment will be made by Second Party to Artist payable thirty days after delivery.

3. Artist agrees to design, execute and produce the limited edition of the Work of Art and Artist shall date, sign, number and affix Artist's copyright notice on each number of the limited edition. Artist shall apply for copyright registration in the name of the Artist and shall retain ownership of the original Work of Art, all incidental work related to the limited edition and all other reproduction and derivative work rights, including merchandising rights, use of title rights, publication rights and foreign edition rights except those covered by this Agreement.

4. Artist agrees to maintain the wholesale and retail prices established by Second Party.

5. The term of the Agreement shall be _____ years from the date of execution or unless sooner terminated.

6. Artist agrees that the Works of Art to be created shall be new and original Works of Art created by the Artist during the term of this Agreement and delivered by the Artist to the Second Party on the following date: _____.

7. Second Party shall have the right, in its reasonable discretion, to accept or reject the finished Work of Art by Artist. In the event that Second Party finds the finished Work unacceptable for any reason, Second Party may request the Artist in writing to make specific changes. If the Artist refuses to make the changes Second Party requests, or if Second Party deems the Work of Art so unsatisfactory that it cannot be made acceptable, Second Party shall have the right in their sole discretion to reject the Work and to request Artist to create an additional new Work of Art during the term of this Agreement. If Second Party finally rejects a Work of Art by the Artist, the Artist reserves all copyright rights and shall have the right to sell or otherwise dispose of it in any way they may choose.

8. Second Party shall have the right to use the Artist's name, portrait and biographical material to publicize and advertise sales of the edition but not as an endorsement of any product or service and likenesses will not be presented to the public in a questionable, undignified or derogatory manner affecting Artist's standing in their profession.

9. The parties agree that during the term of this Agreement, if the Artist creates more than two new and original Works, Second Party shall have the right of first refusal of _____ Works of Art that the Artist creates, on the same terms and conditions as this Agreement provides. Second Party shall not be obligated, however, to accept more than _____ Works during the term of this Agreement.

Nothing in this Agreement is intended to or shall be deemed to create a relationship of employment between the Artist and the Second Party and no Work of Art created by Artist will be a work made for hire.

10. The parties agree that the price and terms of any sale of the individual numbers of the edition(s) covered by this Agreement shall be $_____.

11. Second Party agrees that Artist must receive authorship credit and notice of copyright in artist's name including affixing the copyright symbol, the date and the name of Artist on all reproductions of the Work covered by this Agreement.

12. This Agreement embodies and contains the entire agreement and understandings of the parties and shall be binding upon their respective heirs, legal representatives, successors and assigns.

13. Each party shall take any steps and execute, acknowledge and deliver any further documents that the other may reasonably request to carry out the intent and purpose of this Agreement.

14. This Agreement may not be assigned by Second Party to another person without the prior written consent of the Artist.

15. In any proceeding to enforce any part of this contract, the aggrieved party shall be entitled to reasonable attorney's fees in addition to any available remedy.

16. All notices and other communications shall be in writing and shall be deemed to have been given when delivered or mailed first class, postage prepaid, addressed to the party as set out above, or as they may otherwise designate in writing.

17. This Agreement may be amended, waived, discharged, modified or terminated only by an instrument in writing signed by both parties.

18. Time is of the essence.

19. This Agreement is entered into in the State of _____, contains covenants to be performed within the State of _____ and shall be construed in accordance with and governed by the laws of the State of _____.

20. If the following Special Stipulations conflict with any of the foregoing provisions, the following stipulations are agreed to by the Parties and shall control over any printed portion of this Agreement:

_____

_____

_____

_____

_____

_____

_____

IN WITNESS WHEREOF, the parties have signed this Agreement on the _____ day of

_____, 19_____.

_____ (SEAL)
ARTIST

_____ (SEAL)
SECOND PARTY

LICENSES:

A license grants another person permission to use something that you own. Generally, artists license copyrighted illustrations and designs, occasionally a trademark. A license can be exclusive (meaning only the person you license can use your design) or non-exclusive (meaning you have let more than one person use it) and can extend for any period that the parties agree to. The license agreement is generally used when you are licensing a copyrighted design to be used on a manufactured product. For example, a textile manufacturer may license your design to use on sheets or towels, or a wallpaper manufacturer may want to license your design for a line of wallpaper. It is also used if you have created a product for which you own a registered trademark and you want someone to manufacture the product for you. For example, if you own the trademark on the logo of your business, XYZ Graphics, and you create a sweatshirt for a firm picnic and decide they're commercial enough to sell, you may license an apparel manufacturer to produce them for you.

It is important to understand the difference between a copyright and a trademark. A copyright is the right that you have by virtue of the fact that you created a work of art. The law defines what those rights are, and as the originator of a work and the owner of the copyright, you can decide how to use that work. One thing you may decide to do is license it. A trademark is the right to use a certain design or mark in order to identify some product or service. You own a trademark by virtue of being the first one to identify your product or service with it and by being the first one to register it. Both are valuable assets.

Following are two simple license forms. The first is a simple copyright license form. This is the most common form of licensing for graphic designers. To use this form as the basis for your own agreement, you should: First, decide if you want the license to be exclusive. If you don't, delete the words *sole and exclusive*. Then decide how long you want the license to last—one year, five years, six months—and make sure that is specified. Then make sure that how the design will be used is made clear.

The next form is used to grant permission to use your work for one thing only. For example, if someone wants to use your design on a big sign for an event, use this form.

License Agreement

I, _____, of _____, owner of copyright on

_____, in consideration of _____ dollars paid to me by

_____, grant to _____ a (sole and exclusive) license to use

my copyrighted _____ in _____ for all purposes of

_____ _____ .

_____   _____
(Date)   (Signature)

License (Permission)

Please credit _____, Artist. This Work of Art is furnished to Licensee for the purpose of one-time reproduction but must not be loaned, syndicated or used for advertising or other purpose without prior written permission from Artist.

Artist shall be paid the sum of _____ ($_____) Dollars; Artist reserves all right, title and interest in the Work of Art and all copyright rights. Copyright notice of the copyright symbol, the date and the name of the Artist shall be included on all reproductions.

_____
Artist

_____
Licensee

Purpose and use: _____

_____

_____

MAGAZINE PURCHASE ORDER:

This is a contract between an illustrator and a magazine that can cover many submissions to the magazine over a period of time. It can also be used for individual submissions. If you are selling only one illustration, you can also use the sales contracts or purchase orders in the section "Early-Stage Contracts."

The important points in this contract are:

■ *Rights:* This contract grants the magazine North American rights and not *all rights*. This is significant should the magazine decide to use the drawings in another context (Section 2). It also makes clear that you own the original artwork and that it will be returned (Section 8).

■ *Cancellation:* A kill fee, which protects you in the event the assignment is canceled, is provided for (Section 6). The point at which a kill fee is payable can vary. In this contract, you will be paid a kill fee if the magazine cancels for any reason before you finish the work. After that, the magazine must pay the full fee unless the work is unsatisfactory, in which case you would be paid the kill fee. The earlier the point at which you can get the full fee, the better. But this is a common breakdown.

■ *Copyright Notice:* This contract provides for notice, but does not specify how or where the notice needs to be stated. That's because it varies. Sometimes the notice will be on the illustration; sometimes it will be on the contents page. Generally, the magazine will have a policy regarding placement, but I recommend that notice and credit accompany the art, if possible.

Magazine Purchase Order

(Artist's Letterhead)

This letter is to serve as our contract for me to create certain illustrations for you under the terms described herein.

1. JOB DESCRIPTION. You, the Magazine, retain me, the Illustrator, to create ＿＿＿＿＿＿＿ Illustration(s) described as follows:

＿＿＿＿＿＿＿＿＿＿＿＿＿＿＿＿＿＿＿＿＿＿＿＿＿＿＿＿＿＿＿＿＿＿＿＿＿＿

＿＿＿＿＿＿＿＿＿＿＿＿＿＿＿＿＿＿＿＿＿＿＿＿＿＿＿＿＿＿＿＿＿＿＿＿＿＿

＿＿＿＿＿＿＿＿＿＿＿＿＿＿＿＿＿＿＿＿＿＿＿＿＿＿＿＿＿＿＿＿＿＿＿＿＿＿

to be delivered to the Magazine by ＿＿＿＿＿＿＿＿, 19＿＿, for publication in your magazine titled ＿＿＿＿＿＿＿＿＿＿＿＿＿＿. If sketches are required, they are so noted.

2. GRANT OF RIGHTS. Illustrator hereby agrees to transfer to the Magazine first North American magazine rights in the illustrations. All rights not expressly transferred to the Magazine hereunder are reserved to the Illustrator.

3. PRICE. The Magazine agrees to pay Illustrator the following purchase price: $＿＿＿＿＿＿ in full consideration for Illustrator's grant of rights to Magazine.

4. PAYMENTS. Payment shall be made within thirty (30) days of the billing date.

5. CHANGES. The Illustrator shall be given the first option to make any changes in the work that the Magazine may deem necessary. However, no additional compensation shall be paid unless such changes are necessitated by error or changes in circumstances on the Magazine's part, in which case a new contract between us shall be entered into on mutually agreeable terms to cover changes to be done by the Illustrator.

6. CANCELLATION. If, prior to the Illustrator's completion of finishes, the Magazine cancels the assignment either because the illustrations are unsatisfactory to the Magazine or for any other reason, the Magazine agrees to pay the Illustrator a cancellation fee of 50% of the purchase price. If, after the Illustrator's completion of finishes, the Magazine cancels the assignment, the Magazine agrees to pay 50% of the purchase price if cancellation is due to the illustrations not being reasonably satisfactory and 100% of the purchase price if cancellation is due to any other cause. In the event of cancellation, the Illustrator shall retain ownership of all artwork and rights of copyright, but the Illustrator agrees to show the Magazine the artwork if the Magazine so requests so that the Magazine may make its own evaluation as to degree of completion of the artwork.

7. COPYRIGHT NOTICE AND AUTHORSHIP CREDIT. Copyright notice shall appear in the Illustrator's name with the contribution. The Illustrator shall have the right to receive authorship credit for the illustration and to have such credit removed if the Illustrator so desires due to changes made by the Magazine that are unsatisfactory to the Illustrator.

8. OWNERSHIP OF ARTWORK. The Illustrator shall retain ownership of all original artwork and the Magazine shall return such artwork within thirty (30) days of publication.

To constitute this a binding agreement between us, please sign both copies of this letter and return one copy to me for its files.

_____
ARTIST'S SIGNATURE

_____
MAGAZINE

_____
AUTHORIZED SIGNATURE

_____
NAME AND TITLE

_____
DATE

LATER-STAGE CONTRACTS

These contracts are generally used by established artists with extensive business experience. However, no matter what point you're at, if the contract is appropriate to your needs, use it.

SYNDICATION AGREEMENTS:

A syndicate distributes a group of features on a regular basis to newspapers and other outlets. The most commonly syndicated work is the comic strip. I'm including a sample of a syndication agreement. However, there are many excellent sources of sample syndication agreements along with negotiating tips, and you should consult these if you hope to syndicate a comic strip or have the opportunity to. For example, see *Law and the Writer* (Kirk Polking, Writer's Digest Books).

Each syndicate is different and each artist's needs are different, so you should definitely consult a lawyer if you are asked to sign a syndication agreement. Most are drafted to protect the syndicate. They are always negotiable.

The most famous horror story in the history of cartooning is the story of the creators of Superman. They sold all their rights very early and received very little money from Superman's enormous success. No matter what you think of your strip, it may be the next Superman. So take the syndication contract very seriously.

The most important issues in a syndication contract are:

■ *Term:* The length of a syndication agreement can vary from one to five years. It is better for the artist to sign a contract with as short a term as possible—one or two years.

■ *Payment:* The percentage of the receipts of a strip earned by the artist should be taken against *gross* receipts, not *net* receipts or gross receipts less expenses. Regardless of what percentage you are trying to get (the Cartoonist Guild suggest 50 percent), a minimum payment figure should be included.

Another important payment issue is a percentage to the artist from all subsidiary rights, such as books, television, radio, periodicals, and especially novelty rights. Often a new cartoon can get a high percentage of subsidiary rights (the Guild suggests 75 percent), since no one knows what these sales will amount to yet. Remember, though, that these percentages should also be against *gross* receipts.

■ *Copyright:* If possible, retain the copyright in your cartoon. Require a copyright notice next to your name with publication. This is important with respect to the amount of control you exercise over the material you submit. Keep as much control as you can, requiring approval for changes made in submitted work.

■ *Fees and costs:* A syndication contract will often include various provisions for costs. There may be promotional costs, legal fees, or other types of costs to the publisher or the artist. Make sure it is clear who pays for what. Legal fees should be evenly divided. If there is to be a promotional campaign (and many cartoonists feel that this is critical to the success of a strip), be sure it is clear who pays the cost of it, and whether the right to use the cartoon in promotional materials will be additionally compensated.

Other Important Dos And Don'ts in a Syndication Contract:

■ Do not give up the right to sell other work elsewhere. If a publisher wants *all* your work, it should cost much more.

■ Do not give the syndicate the right to future work. You may be able to command more money later.

■ Do not sell more than one cartoon strip in one contract. Each strip should be negotiated separately.

■ Do include the right to inspect books and records or get a periodic accounting.

■ Do not allow all proceeds from the strip to revert to the syndicate in the event of your death. Your heirs should receive the money.

■ Do provide for the return of original art. It cuts down on unauthorized use.

Sample Syndicate Agreement

Agreement made this day of _____ between _____ (herein known as the syndicate) and _____ (herein known as the creator).

SYNDICATION

During the term of this agreement the syndicate shall make reasonable efforts to sell the feature to newspapers and shall take other action, if necessary, to exploit the feature in newspapers and magazines as the syndicate deems appropriate. The syndicate shall have the right to determine prices and terms of sale in any media.

FEATURE

The creator agrees to prepare and furnish to the syndicate installments of _____, (herein known as the feature). The creator agrees to furnish during this agreement material of a quality equal to that of the material heretofore submitted and of a standard consistent with the requirements of the syndicate.

The feature shall be delivered to the syndicate at a place to be designated by the syndicate. The expense of the transmission of the feature to such place shall be borne by the creator.

Each installment of the feature shall be delivered to the syndicate at such a time as the syndicate may reasonably request; inasmuch as the syndicate is obligated to deliver the feature to its customers regularly and at fixed times and as failure to make such regular and timely delivery might subject the syndicate to liability, it is expressly agreed that the time for delivery of installments of the feature to the syndicate shall be of the essence of this agreement. The creator shall indemnify the syndicate against any damage (including reasonable attorney's fees) caused by any failure to make such regular and timely delivery. The syndicate shall have the right, at its election, to select counsel to defend any claim, suit or action. The syndicate has the right to hire writers or artists to prepare the installments of the feature on the creator's behalf, should the creator not make timely delivery of the installments of the feature, and the costs and expenses incurred by the syndicate to obtain substitute writers and artists to prepare installments of the feature shall be borne by the creator.

The creator warrants that all work produced by him under this contract, including the names, characters, plot or plan and subject matter thereof, shall be new and original, that the publication thereof or the exercise of any right herein granted to the syndicate with respect thereto shall not in any way infringe upon the copyright, trademark, trade name or literary, artistic or other property right of any person, firm or corporation, and that the creator is bound by an existing contract that would hinder or prevent his performance of the obligations assumed by him hereunder. The creator further warrants that the work that he produces under this contract shall not contain any libelous or unlawful matter. In case any dispute, controversy or litigation arises between the syndicate and any person, firm, or corporation based upon or growing out of the contention that said work produced by the creator under this contract, or the name, title, characters, plot or plan or subject matter thereof infringes upon the rights of any person, firm, or corporation, or that the same contains any libelous or unlawful matter, it is agreed that the creator will indemnify the syndicate against any damages (including reasonable attorney's fees) incurred in such connection. The creator shall not be liable, under the provisions of this paragraph for any changes or revisions made by the syndicate in any work produced by the creator under the terms of this agreement.

The syndicate shall not be obliged to accept, syndicate or pay for any installments of the feature which do not comply with requirements set forth herein, or which, in the syndicate's reasonable opinion, might subject the syndicate to any claim by a third party.

EXCLUSIVITY

During the term of this agreement, the creator agrees that he will not, without the written consent of the syndicate, produce a similar feature for newspapers or any other periodical or magazine produced or distributed as part of any newspaper. The creator acknowledges that in the case of such breach of such covenant, the syndicate shall be entitled to equitable relief.

OWNERSHIP

The creator acknowledges that the syndicate is the owner of the feature and the syndicate shall be owner of all installments of the feature as well as all subsidiary rights therein (including, but not limited to, publication rights, stage, motion picture, radio, television, mechanical reproduction and any commercial exploitation rights) and that the syndicate's rights include without limitation, the exclusive right to publish the feature in newspapers throughout the world. The syndicate shall also have the exclusive right (but not obligation) to obtain and maintain trademarks, trade mark registration and copyrights of or relating to such installments of the feature, in the syndicate's name or such other name or names that the syndicate may elect, and to obtain renewals thereof. Creator agrees to execute and deliver to the syndicate, promptly on request, any documents that evidence the syndicate's exclusive rights provided herein or assist the syndicate to obtain and protect trademarks, copyrights and similar rights.

COMPENSATION

In consideration of the satisfactory performance by the creator of his obligations hereunder, the syndicate shall pay to the creator at approximately monthly (four or five week intervals):

Fifty percent of the syndicate's net collections from the sale for publication in newspapers, newspaper supplements and like periodicals of the rights to use the name, title, characters or substance of any material produced by the creator hereunder; and

Fifty percent of the syndicate's net collections, derived after deduction from the gross collections of all of the syndicate's expenses in connection therewith, from the sale for all other purposes of said rights.

The syndicate shall keep accurate books and records reflecting amounts accrued from the sale of the feature and shall furnish to the creator upon his request statements which shall disclose all sales of the feature, the purchasers and the amounts actually received. The creator shall have the right to examine the syndicate's records in which the accounts and information relative to this agreement are maintained, provided such inspection shall be made during business hours and upon reasonable notice.

TERM OF AGREEMENT

The term of this agreement shall begin on the date hereof and shall end on the __(number of years)__ annual anniversary date of the date of the first publication of the feature hereunder subject to (a) earlier termination as provided for in the section Termination hereof or, (b) renewal as provided herein.

The term of this agreement shall be automatically renewed and extended for __(number)__ period of __(number)__ years upon the same terms and conditions set forth herein, unless the syndicate gives written notice at least 60 days before the termination date of the initial period, that the agreement shall not be renewed and extended.

The creator recognizes that the publication of the feature will greatly enhance the value of the feature and that the syndicate is entitled to protection against the loss of its investment of money and promotional effort in the feature which would result from the transfer of the creator's services in connection with the feature to another syndicate or agency at the end of the term of this agreement. Accordingly, the creator agrees that the syndicate shall have the first right of refusal to contract with the creator for the creator's services in connection with the feature after the second __(number of years)__ term. The creator agrees that ninety days prior to the end of the term of this agreement, the creator will first negotiate with the syndicate for continuation of his services in connection with the syndication and exploitation rights to the feature before negotiating with any other person or firm.

TERMINATION OF AGREEMENT

If for any six week period during the term of this agreement, thirty days after first publication of the feature in newspapers under this agreement, the average weekly gross receipts shall be less than $_____, the syndicate or the creator may terminate this agreement.

If the feature is not published in any newspaper before __(date)__ , this agreement is null and void.

In the event of the termination of this agreement otherwise than by the death of the creator, all compensation payable by the syndicate shall cease to accrue as of the date of such event, except for an amount equal to fifty percent of the gross collections from the first, second and future publication in newspapers, newspaper supplements and like periodicals of material furnished to the syndicate prior to the date of such termination and published for the first time thereafter. In the event of the termination of this contract due to the death of the creator and the syndicate determines to continue publication in the newspapers, newspaper supplements and like periodicals or exploitation of the subsidiary rights relating to the feature containing the name, characters or substance of the material produced by the creator hereunder, the syndicate shall pay to the creator, his heirs or assigns, for each year after the creator's death during which the syndicate shall continue such publication or exploitation, amounts equal to fifty percent of the net collections from the sale for publication or exploitation. Net receipts are defined as gross collections less expenses incurred by the syndicate relating to the publication or exploitation of the feature, the name, the title, characters or substance of the feature produced by the creator as covered by this agreement.

USE OF NAME

The creator hereby grants to the syndicate, its subscribers, appointees, licensees and successors, the right to use his name and picture for promotion, trade and advertising purposes.

RIGHT TO EDIT FEATURE

The syndicate shall have the entire editorial supervision of the feature and may make changes, alterations, revisions, deletions or additions to the feature or any installment thereof.

ASSIGNMENT

The syndicate may assign its rights and obligations under this agreement to any other corporation or other entity which succeeds to acquire substantially all the business and assets of the syndicate.

GENERAL

The section headings contained herein are for reference purposes only and shall not in any way affect the meaning or interpretation of this agreement.

In witness whereof, the parties have executed this agreement as of the date shown above.

_____

Artist's Signature

_____

Syndicate

_____

Authorized Signature

_____

Date

From *How to Make Money in Newspaper Syndication*, pages 37-41, ©1985 by Susan Lane. Used by permission of Newspaper Syndication Specialists.

AGENT OR REPRESENTATIVE CONTRACT:

It is generally at the later stages of your career that you make a decision about whether to have someone represent you. Your relationship with an artist's rep can be fraught with legal peril. Conflicts generally arise over money—whether your rep is entitled to it or whether you're getting enough of it or whether you're getting it on time. They also arise over whether the rep is doing enough to promote the artist's work. This is an area where differing expectations cause problems. Enter it carefully. Do not let anyone represent you without a written contract.

The following is a standard rep contract. But rep contracts are very personal. No one contract will suit everyone.

This contract should be used as a guide to the major terms. It clearly sets out the terms of the relationship. In Section 2, the contract deals with promotional expenses and basically splits them between the artist and the agent. It provides for the agent to pay for shipping and insurance. Make sure this section is clear about who pays for what. Commissions under this agreement (Section 4) are fairly standard. It is important to remember that under this contract, you will pay your representative 10 percent of any work you get on your own while you have this agreement *and* for any work that someone else who is listed in this agreement gets for you. No commissions are paid on rejected work or work for which you don't get paid. In addition—and this is critical—this contract provides that you deduct your expenses *before* you calculate the commissions.

Billing is also an important issue in artist-rep relationships. This contract gives you the option of who does the billing (Section 5). If you do the billing, you also have the bookkeeping responsibility and hassle. If you can handle it, do the billing. If not, the contract protects you in the event you have difficulty getting your money from the rep.

Agent-Artist Agreement

AGREEMENT, this _____ day of _____, 19____, between

_____ (hereinafter referred to as the "Artist"), residing at

_____

and _____ (hereinafter referred to as the "Agent"), residing at

_____.

WHEREAS, the Artist is an established artist of proven abilities; and

WHEREAS, the Artist wishes to have an agent represent him or her in marketing certain rights enumerated herein; and

WHEREAS, the Agent is capable of marketing the artwork produced by the Artist; and

WHEREAS, the Agent wishes to represent the Artist;

NOW, THEREFORE, in consideration of the foregoing promises and the mutual covenants hereinafter set forth and other valuable consideration, the parties hereto agree as follows:

1. AGENCY. The Artist appoints the Agent to act as his or her exclusive representative: (A) in the following geographical area: _____

_____

_____

(B) for the markets listed here (specify publishing, advertising, etc.): _____

_____

_____

The Agent agrees to use his or her best efforts in submitting the Artist's work for the purpose of securing assignment for the Artist. The Agent shall negotiate the terms of any assignment that is offered, but the Artist shall have the right to reject any assignment if he or she finds the terms thereof unacceptable.

2. PROMOTION. The Artist shall provide the Agent with such samples of work as are from time to time necessary for the purpose of securing assignments. These samples shall remain the property of the Artist and be returned on Termination of this Agreement. The Agent shall take reasonable efforts to protect the work from loss or damage, but shall be liable for such loss or damage only if caused by the Agent's negligence. Promotional expenses, including but not limited to promotional mailings and paid advertising, shall be paid _____% by the Agent and _____% by the Artist. The Agent shall bear the expenses of shipping and insurance.

3. TERM. This Agreement shall take effect on the _____ day of _____,

19_____, and remain in full force and effect for a term of one year, unless terminated as provided in Paragraph 9.

4. COMMISSIONS. The Agent shall be entitled to the following commissions: (A) On assignments incurred by the Agent during the term of this Agreement, twenty-five (25%) percent of the billing. (B) On house accounts, ten (10%) percent of the billing. For purposes of this Agreement, *house accounts* are defined as accounts obtained by the Artist at any time or obtained by another agent representing the Artist prior to the commencement of this Agreement and are listed below:

_____

_____

It is understood by both parties that no commissions shall be paid on assignments rejected by the Artist or for which the Artist fails to receive payment, regardless of the reason payment is not made. Further, no commissions shall be payable in either (A) or (B) above for any part of the billing that is due to expenses incurred by the Artist in performing the assignment, whether or not such expenses are reimbursed by the client. In the event that a flat fee is paid by the client, it shall be reduced by the amount of expenses incurred by the Artist in performing the assignment, and the Agent's commission shall be payable only on the fee as reduced for expenses.

5. BILLING. The _____ Artist _____ Agent shall be responsible for all billings.

6. PAYMENTS. The party responsible for billing shall make all payments due within ten (10) days of receipt of any fees covered by this Agreement. Late payments shall be accompanied by interest calculated at the rate of _____% per month thereafter.

7. ACCOUNTINGS. The party responsible for billing shall send copies of invoices to the other party when rendered. If requested, that party shall also provide the other party with semi-annual accountings showing all assignments for the period, the clients' names, the fees paid, expenses incurred by the Artist, the dates of payment, the amounts on which the Agent's commissions are to be calculated, and the sums due less those amounts already paid.

8. INSPECTION OF THE BOOKS AND RECORDS. The party responsible for the billing shall keep the books and records with respect to commissions due at his or her place of business and permit the other party to inspect these books and records during normal business hours on the giving of reasonable notice.

9. TERMINATION. This Agreement may be terminated by either party by giving thirty (30) days written notice to the other party. If the Artist receives assignments after the termination date from clients originally obtained by the Agent during the term of this Agreement, the commission specified in Paragraph 4(A) shall be payable to the Agent under the following circumstances. If the Agent has

represented the Artist for six months or less, the Agent shall receive a commission on such assignments received by the Artist within ninety (90) days of the date of termination. This period shall increase by thirty (30) days for each additional six months that the Agent has represented the Artist, but in no event shall such period exceed one hundred eighty (180) days.

10. ASSIGNMENT. This Agreement shall not be assigned by either of the parties hereto. It shall be binding on and inure to the benefit of the successors, administrators, executors, or heirs of the Agent and Artist.

11. NOTICES. All notices shall be given to the parties at their respective addresses set forth above.

12. INDEPENDENT CONTRACTOR STATUS. Both parties agree that the Agent is acting as an independent contractor. This Agreement is not an employment agreement, nor does it constitute a joint venture or partnership between the Artist and Agent.

13. AMENDMENTS AND MERGER. All amendments to this Agreement must be written. This Agreement incorporates the entire understanding of the parties.

14. GOVERNING LAW. This Agreement shall be governed by the laws of the State of

_____.

    IN WITNESS WHEREOF, the parties have signed this Agreement as of the date set forth above.

_____
ARTIST

_____
AGENT

TRADEMARK LICENSE:

A trademark license agreement is needed when you own a registered trademark and want someone to manufacture something for you. This agreement contains the major structure of this type of agreement but agreements themselves vary considerably with every arrangement. It creates a royalty arrangement (Section 5) as compensation to you for the use of your mark and contains a number of ways that you, as the trademark owner, can control how your mark is used (Sections 2, 3, and 4). Trademark licensing, however, is complicated. If you are contemplating such an arrangement, I would recommend consulting an attorney.

Trademark License

This License Agreement entered into, effective as of _____ day of

_____, 19_____, by and between Artist, having a principal place of business at

_____, (hereinafter called LICENSOR): and _____, a

Corporation organized and existing under the Laws of the State of _____, and

having a principal place of business at _____, (hereinafter called LICENSEE).

WITNESSETH:

WHEREAS, Licensor is the creator of _____, having designed and developed

same and having established a market for the same using the trademark _____;

and

WHEREAS, Licensee desires to obtain license rights to make _____, in

accordance with the specifications of Licensor and thereafter market the same under the Trademark

_____;

NOW, THEREFORE, it is mutually agreed as follows:

1. GRANT: Licensor hereby grants to Licensee the right to use the aforementioned Trademark in

connection with the aforementioned _____, but only so long as

_____ are manufactured in accordance with the specifications established by

Licensor.

2. QUALITY CONTROL: Licensor will provide detailed specifications to Licensee which relate to the

materials for and the manufacture of _____. Licensor will have the unqualified

right, at any and all reasonable times, and without prior notice to inspect the materials and

manufacturing processes employed by Licensee in the manufacture of _____.

3. MARKING: Licensee shall mark the _____, with a suitable legend, in a

form approved in advance by Licensor, indicating that the _____ is made under

License.

4. ADVERTISING: Licensee shall submit to Licensor, for prior approval, all of Licensee's proposed

advertising with respect to _____ license to be sold under the aforementioned

Trademark.

5. ROYALTY: As consideration for the license granted hereunder, Licensee agrees to pay Licensor

the sum of $_____ of Licensee's net selling price of $_____. License fees hereunder

shall be remitted monthly and Licensee shall keep sufficient and accurate books and records to enable

verification of the amount due under this Agreement.

6. TERMINATION: This Agreement will have an initial term of _____ years, and shall automatically be renewed at the options of Licensee, for successive _____ years, provided, however, that (a) Licensee gives ninety (90) days' prior notice of intent to renew and (b) Licensee shall have no right of renewal if Licensee is in breach or default ninety (90) days prior to the end of a _____ year term.

IN WITNESS WHEREOF, the parties have executed this Agreement effective as of the date first written above.

_____

ARTIST'S SIGNATURE

_____

XYZ CORPORATION

MISCELLANEOUS CONTRACTS

This section contains two contracts that may be useful but do not fit into one of the previous categories. They are a licensing representative agreement and a model release form.

LICENSE REPRESENTATIVE LETTER AGREEMENT:

This agreement is similar to an artist's representative agreement (see page 96). The difference is that a licensing representative's job is to find ways to *license* your art, design, or trademark and negotiate the use of those licenses rather than just sell your work. It outlines the terms of the agreement based on a percentage for the rep (Section 3) and protects your copyright (Section 8). The most important thing it does, though, is make clear that only authorized expenses may be deducted from royalty payments (Section 5).

Licensing Representative
Letter Agreement

From: Artist _____

Address: _____

Date: _____

To: _____

Address: _____

Dear Licensing Representative:

This is to confirm that I agree for you to be my licensing representative on the following terms:

1. You will use your best efforts to seek out and submit to me potential licensees of my work(s) of art, trademarks, trade names, designs and know-how, and to negotiate with any potential licensees on my behalf. All transactions shall be subject to my prior written approval. Any inquiry received by me during the term of this agreement from any potential licensee will be referred to you.

2. If I enter into any agreement with a licensee either (i) during the term of this Agreement, or (ii) after the term of this Agreement with a person, corporation or entity with whom negotiation was started during the term, then you will be entitled to the commission provided.

3. Your commission will be equal to _____% of my royalties and receipts from licenses for the duration, and for the duration of any renewals and/or extensions.

4. You will bill the licensees for total royalties, deduct your commission, and remit the balance to me monthly. In order to facilitate billings, I will deliver to you copies of all applicable reports of sales promptly after my receipt of any reports.

5. You will pay for all of your own expenses, unless specifically approved in advance by me in connection with collecting royalties, or for long distance telephone calls made in connection with my business. I will only reimburse you for long distance, travel and living expenses incurred by you in connection with my business if you have my prior written approval.

6. This Agreement shall commence on _____, 19_____, and shall continue in effect for a period of _____ (_____) years, with automatic _____ (_____) year renewals unless terminated by either of us upon notice given to the other at least sixty (60) days prior to the then current expiration date. If you fail to secure any royalty-producing agreements for me by _____, 19_____, this

Agreement may be cancelled by either of us upon thirty (30) days' notice given on or before

_____, 19_____.

7. You will render monthly accountings to me as to royalties collected by you, commissions earned, and approved expenses charged. Accountings will be submitted by the fifteenth (15th) day of every month with respect to the preceding month. I may, upon reasonable notice and during regular business hours, examine your books to verify the sums due.

8. This Agreement is not intended to nor does it transfer any rights of copyright to licensing representative.

9. This Agreement cannot be amended, discharged, or terminated orally. All notices shall be in writing. This Agreement shall be governed and construed solely by the laws of the State of _____. Time is of the essence.

If the foregoing correctly states our entire understanding, please sign and return a copy of this letter to me, constituting this a binding agreement between us.

_____   _____
LICENSING REPRESENTATIVE   ARTIST

From *Contracts for Artists*, p. 61 ©
1982 by William R. Gignilliat. Used by
permission of the author.

MODEL RELEASE FORM:

Any time you use models, have them sign a release form. If you have any doubt as to whether a release is required, get one. This applies to photographs as well as paintings and drawings. It applies to somebody's house or garden. It applies to clearly recognizable people in a crowd and to any objects that are owned by someone else. Make copies of this form and keep them handy.

Model Release

I (We), _____ (model's name) _____ being of legal age hereby consent and authorize

_____ (artist's name) _____, successors, legal representatives and assigns to use and reproduce a

photograph(s) taken by _____ (artist's name) _____ on _____ (date) _____ and to reproduce my name (or

any fictional name), photograph, picture or portrait in all forms and media, for any and all purposes

including publication and advertising of every description. No claim of any kind will be made by me.

No representations have been made to me.

I hereby warrant that I am of legal age and have every right to contract in my own name; that I

have read the above authorization and release prior to its execution and that I am fully familiar with

its contents.

_____   _____
Date   Witness

_____   _____
Name   Address

_____
Address

Reprinted by permission of *The Artist's Magazine* © 1987.

WHAT TO DO IF YOU DON'T GET PAID

If you have completed work for someone and they haven't paid you for it after you have billed them for a while, you have several options:

■ If you are required to do any more work, refuse to do it until you get paid.

■ If the amount is relatively low, under five hundred dollars, you can file a complaint in small claims court.

■ If the amount is higher, see a lawyer. If you have used a form of the contracts in this book, your lawyer will have very little trouble getting your money for you. If you have no contract, it will be much harder, but not necessarily impossible.

Letters and phone calls are the traditional ways of trying to get paid. I would recommend waiting only sixty days and then taking some kind of legal action. My experience has been that the longer you wait to get paid, the less likely you will get paid without taking some kind of action.

One way to avoid this situation is to know whom you are working for. Check out the businesses you deal with. Find out how long they have been around. Talk to people who have worked for them. If you have reservations about whether or not you will get paid, don't do the work. It is better not to work and not get paid than to work and not get paid.

CONCLUSION

The most important thing to remember about contracts is that they are designed to help you. It is for your protection that arrangements regarding your work be put in writing. Whether you use a formal contract, a letter, a sales receipt, or an invoice, write it down.

The contracts in this book provide enough material to put together an agreement for almost any type of work. Take the time to create your own contract for the type of transactions you generally engage in, and then use it.

COMMONLY ASKED QUESTIONS: CONTRACTS

Q. *About a year ago, I was commissioned to paint a portrait. I was paid in full for the work. Now, the customer decides he doesn't like it and wants his money back. What should I do?*

A. If you have a contract for the commission of the work, it should say that final payment constitutes approval of the work by the commissioning party. Whether or not you have a contract, you do not have to return the money. Explain to your former customer that you considered his final payment to constitute his approval of the work, that commissioned work is not returnable, and that you will take the portrait back but will not refund the money. If he sues you for the money and you do not have a contract, you will have a more difficult time with the case than you would if you had a contract. But the burden of proving that he's entitled to the return of his money is his.

Q. *What does it mean when a gallery states that "exclusive area representation" is required? Should I agree to it?*

A. *Exclusive area representation* means that the gallery is the only one who can sell your work within a particular area, usually a city or a state. Anyone who wants to buy your work must buy it through that gallery. Exclusive arrangements are very common. You should agree to it as long as the other terms of the arrangement—percentages, timely payment, length of time of the agreement—are to your satisfaction.

Q. *I'm getting paid only $10 for an illustration. Why should I bother with a contract or invoice? Anyway, the art director resents all these fancy invoices and contracts.*

A. You should bother with an invoice because it protects your reproduction rights in case the art director decides to use your $10 illustration on something else. The art director's resentment is his problem. Yours is to protect yourself and your work.

Q. *How specific and descriptive should a contract be? Artwork is often a very subjective and interpretive thing. What I think looks good and what the client wants may turn out to be two different things. How can you prove you have met all the criteria in your original agreement if the art director thinks you haven't?*

A. There's no such thing as a contract that is too specific or too descriptive, especially in an area as subjective as artwork. You cannot "prove" you have met all the criteria in your original agreement if an art director thinks you haven't. But you have a much better chance of convincing the art director or a court if the description is clearly written down.

Q. *The gallery that represents me went bankrupt, and my paintings were sold to pay the bills. I did not agree to this. What can I do?*

A. It depends on what state you live in. Some states have consignment statutes that protect you in a situation like this. In any case, see an attorney.

Q. *I recently received $10 for an illustration when I was supposed to be paid $20. I have an invoice as evidence. What can I do?*

A. Call. Write letters. If you are not paid in six months, forget it. Amounts under $100 are generally not worth the expense of fighting for.

Q. *I signed a consignment contract with a gallery in another state. I never visited the gallery because it was so far away. It's been two and a half years since I signed with them, and I have never heard whether I made a sale. I have tried calling, and all I get is a secretary who says the director will call back—he never does. My letters have not been answered either. What should I do? Can I get my paintings back?*

A. It depends on what your contract says. A good consignment agreement would not last longer than a year, would provide for access to books and records to determine sales, and would provide for the return of all work at termination of the agreement at someone's expense. You can get your paintings back. But you will probably have to go to the gallery and get them yourself.

Q. *The art director of a magazine called me and asked me to illustrate a piece on traffic safety. The art director sent a contract along with some directions for the piece. I completed the piece on time and to his liking. However, the piece was pulled from the magazine and was never used. Don't I get paid at least for my efforts?*

A. It depends on your contract. A good one will include a kill fee.

Q. *Can I ever get rights to a piece I did as work made for hire?*

A. Yes, you can buy them back or include them as compensation in another deal with your employer.

Q. *I want to paint a beach scene from a photograph I took. Do I need a model release?*

A. Yes. If there are recognizable people in any picture you are painting from, get releases.

Q. *I illustrated a book for a book publisher. The publisher wants to use one of my illustrations for promotional purposes. Is this a regular practice? Should I be compensated for this?*

A. Yes, it is a common practice, and yes, you should be compensated.

EASY REFERENCE CHECK-LISTS: CONTRACTS

All contracts must include these elements:
- [ ] Parties—At least two people are needed for a legal contract.
- [ ] Consent—Both parties must agree to the terms.
- [ ] Consideration—Money or some other payment is necessary.
- [ ] Obligation—Some action must be required in exchange for the consideration.

Some simple contracts are:
- [ ] A letter of agreement
- [ ] An invoice or bill of sale
- [ ] A typed form stating all terms

Some important contract terms for an artist or graphic artist are:
- [ ] Amount of payment
- [ ] Manner and time frame of payment, such as "Payment is a flat fee due within days of completion of the project."
- [ ] Who pays what expenses
- [ ] What reproduction rights have been purchased
- [ ] Delivery time
- [ ] What happens if the project is killed or the artwork deemed unsatisfactory
- [ ] Complete description of job
- [ ] Terms for return of original artwork
- [ ] Whether you are a freelance artist or are considered an employee

What to do if you don't get paid:
- [ ] Refuse to do further work if asked.
- [ ] Send copies of your invoice to the buyer.
- [ ] After sending invoice copies, warn the buyer that you will take further legal action.
- [ ] If the amount is small, file a complaint in small claims court.
- [ ] If the amount is substantial, see a lawyer.

CHAPTER 4
RECORDKEEPING AND TAXES

By Floyd Conner

Recordkeeping may be one of the least enjoyable tasks related to being an artist, but it is also one of the most important. At first glance, recordkeeping may seem like nothing more than a time-consuming practice, but proper recordkeeping can actually save time, not to mention anguish and money when tax season rolls around.

Good recordkeeping can improve your spending habits, making it less likely that you will let money slip through your fingers. It also allows you to keep a record of the status of your business. It can help you determine what prices you can hope to charge for your work in the future. By consulting your records, you can see if you are asking enough for your work to make a profit.

And it assists you in maintaining proper tax records. The Internal Revenue Service requires that you keep books and records that are adequate for audit purposes. The law requires that as a businessperson, you keep records that are both accurate and systematic.

Along with the need for good recordkeeping goes the need for a thorough understanding of tax law. The Tax Reform Act of 1986 was the most comprehensive tax legislation since World War II. While the main purpose of this act was to simplify the tax system and lower the tax rate for most individuals, the elimination of many deductions and credits has resulted in some persons' actually having to pay higher taxes.

Many of the new tax laws have a direct effect on you as an artist. For example, a new law makes it necessary for artists to keep

separate records of the art materials used on each individual project. If you take a home office deduction, as many artists do, then you must maintain separate business and personal records for your household.

In this chapter, I'll highlight the new tax laws as well as suggest better ways you can keep your business records. I'll discuss various recordkeeping systems and suggest which may be the best for you. Then I'll explain all the important tax changes, placing special emphasis on those that directly affect artists. I'll go over how to complete your tax return, including how to fill out Schedules C and SE, and how to compute self-employment tax. We'll discuss the pros and cons of the home office deduction and ways to improve your chances of coming out ahead after an audit.

By understanding the new tax laws and maintaining a proper bookkeeping system, you can reduce your taxes and prevent costly errors. And it may be easier than you think.

RECORDKEEPING

Your recordkeeping system can be as simple or as complex as your needs dictate. If your finances are too complicated or time-consuming for you to handle, then you would be wise to turn your books over to an accountant. But in most cases, you can save money and do it yourself. And once a proper bookkeeping system is established, you will be surprised how little time and effort is required each day to keep your records up to date.

What's Needed
Your records should identify all sources of income and deductible expenses related to your profession. The records should be accurate, standardized, and simple enough that you can easily locate anything you're looking for.

Though it is essential that you be able to

Floyd Conner is a tax specialist and author who lives in Cincinnati, Ohio. He has written a handbook on taxes for the Internal Revenue Service, where he is employed. He has also written books on sports and has published numerous magazine articles on a variety of topics.

completely understand your records, it is also important that they be accessible to others. While the Internal Revenue Service does not care what recordkeeping system you use, it does insist that your records be made available to them whenever a discrepancy occurs, so it is important to maintain clear, legible, and complete records. The Internal Revenue Service places the burden of proof on you to support any deduction you claim. This might be the IRS's way of saying that you're guilty until proven innocent. If an IRS agent concludes that your business records are inadequate or misleading, you may be warned, fined, and even prosecuted if it is suspected that there was a criminal intent to avoid taxes.

While such drastic action is rare, it's in your best interest to keep accurate and permanent records. Proper and complete records of your business transactions remove any suspicions the IRS may have of willful negligence in reporting your taxes. It will be an indication of your professionalism, which could be a determining factor in your favor if the IRS ever questions whether your art is a business.

I'll discuss the different types of recordkeeping systems later, but first you need to make several important decisions about your art and your accounting needs.

Hobby or Business?

One of the first determinations you'll need to make is whether your art is a hobby or a business. Bo Jackson may consider professional football to be a hobby, but you probably consider yourself to be a professional artist. Whether the IRS considers you to be a professional or a hobbyist depends on your ability to show a profit. One of the major changes of the 1986 Tax Reform Act was that a self-employed individual has to show a profit three out of five consecutive years for his work to be considered a business. Under the old law, it was necessary to make a profit in just two of five consecutive years.

If you cannot meet this requirement, the Internal Revenue Service presumes that you are not in business with a profit motive; therefore your artistic endeavor will be considered a hobby instead of a business. What makes this distinction so important is that if you're engaged in a business, you can deduct all ordinary and necessary business expenses, even if they exceed your income. In other words, you are permitted to take a loss on your business activity.

Unfortunately, if you show a loss in three of five consecutive years, then the burden of proving a profit motive rests on your shoulders. However, if the reverse is true and you have made a profit in at least three of five consecutive years, then the burden of proof rests with the IRS.

In some instances, you may benefit by filing Form 5213, Election to Postpone Determination With Respect to the Presumption That an Activity Is Engaged in for Profit, with the IRS. By filing this form, you can postpone for up to five years any determination by the Internal Revenue Service concerning your profit motive. This stalling maneuver can give you some extra time to establish a profitable business; it can be especially helpful for the young artist just starting out. The drawback of this procedure is that it may alert the IRS to the possibility that your business may not be a consistent money maker.

If the IRS challenges your profit motive, you are given the opportunity to prove your professionalism. You must present convincing evidence that you should be considered a professional artist and that you conduct your business with the intention of making a profit. There are nine factors the Internal Revenue considers in determining whether you should be classified for tax purposes as a hobbyist or a professional.

The Manner in Which You Conduct Your Business If you conduct your profession in a businesslike manner, then the IRS will likely presume that you are pursuing it for profit. You can demonstrate a businesslike manner in several ways. One of the best ways is to maintain complete and accurate records. You can also demonstrate your profit motive by being actively involved in marketing your work, showing in galleries, and other businesslike practices associated with being a professional artist. Even relatively minor things such as having a business card or business stationery can indicate to the IRS that you are pursuing your profession with the intention of making a profit. Memberships in professional organizations may also be construed as businesslike behavior.

The Expertise of the Artist Another point in your favor will be if you display expertise in your field. If you have had formal training as an artist or possess academic credentials that certify you as an expert, then this will be looked on favorably by the IRS. Even if you are a self-taught artist, you can subscribe to art journals on a regular basis to indicate that you are keeping up with new techniques in the art world and are intending to use that knowledge to make a profit. Naturally, if you have instructed others on the subject as a teacher, then this will imply a certain expertise. Another sign of expertise is having received critical recognition of your work. A testimonial from a respected artist or critic would also carry some weight with the IRS.

The Amount of Time and Effort Expended by the Artist The time and effort that you devote to your art is an important factor in the IRS's decision as to whether you are a professional or a hobbyist. If your art is a full-time venture and your primary source of income, then it should be apparent to the IRS that it is your profession and not just a hobby. After all, by definition, a *hobby* is something that someone likes to do in her spare time. Another sign of your sincerity would be if you abandoned a profitable occupation to pursue your artistic career full time, or if over a period of time you have gradually been devoting more time to your artwork.

Expectation of Future Profits If you are not currently making a profit as an artist but have reason to believe that you will be in the near future, then this should indicate professional intent on your part. For most artists, it takes years to establish a reputation and clientele. If your sales have steadily increased, then this would warrant a reasonable expectation of future profits. So would pointing out that your work is selling at a higher price. This situation not only increases your profit margin, but it also suggests that the price of your work will continue to go up in value. Logically, unsold art still in your possession should also appreciate in value as your reputation grows. Another approach you might take is to argue that the present market for your work is not as great as it will be in the future. You will need to present evidence to support that claim. For example, if your style is in a state of transition, then this may explain temporary losses.

Success in Similar Ventures If you have been successful in similar ventures, then you are more likely to be successful in your present endeavor. The IRS might also be impressed if you have been a success in an unrelated venture, because past success could indicate that in whatever line of work you pursue, you intend and have the ability to make a profit.

Your History of Profit and Losses The IRS understands that as an artist, you cannot be expected to make a profit in your start-up year. However, if your losses continue over a period of years or get larger every year, then your profit motive is sure to be questioned. Two indicators the IRS will be looking at are if your receipts have been increasing in recent years and if your losses have been decreasing and becoming less frequent.

The Amount of Occasional Profits In the past, if you have occasionally shown a profit, then in all likelihood your business will be profitable at some time in the future. The larger the profit in a particular year, the stronger the case you have with the IRS. For example, if in the last five years you had three years with small losses and two years with substantial gains, then it would be viewed more favorably by the IRS than if you had three years of substantial losses and two years of small profits. Remember that the expectation of profit does not have to be reasonable, it merely needs to be made in good faith.

Your Financial Status If you have other sources of income and you show persistent losses from your art, then the IRS will have reason to believe that it's only a hobby. The IRS may believe that you're simply taking a loss to avoid paying taxes on other income. Conversely, if you have no other substantial source of income, then the IRS has no reason to doubt your profit motive. For once, being a starving artist can have its advantages.

Elements of Personal Pleasure or Recreation The IRS does not expect you to suffer for your art. As far as they're concerned, you can enjoy yourself all you want, just as long as your primary motive is profit. In fact, if you enjoy what you're doing, then you're more likely to be a success, and the more successful you become, the more you enjoy what you're doing. For most artists, their art represents their means of expression. Just as long as it's also a means of earning a living, the IRS will not question your motivation.

Review all these factors carefully and determine whether your artwork should be considered a hobby or a business. This determination will be important as you decide what kind of records to keep.

Accounting Periods

The next decision you'll need to make is what accounting period you'll use. You don't have to be an accountant to understand the accounting period. It is simply the time frame you'll use to report income and claim deductions. Most likely you will elect a *calendar-year accounting period*. As the name suggests, a calendar-year accounting period begins on January 1 and ends on December 31. An accounting period other than a calendar year is known as a *fiscal year*.

If you are starting up your business in the middle of the year, that doesn't mean you have to use a fiscal year as your accounting period. For the first year, you may use a short tax year, one that lasts less than twelve months. If you ever need to change your accounting period, it will be necessary to file Form 1128, Application for Change in Accounting Period, with the IRS.

Accounting Methods

Once you've selected your accounting period, you'll need to determine which accounting method best suits your business. Your accounting method will determine what income and expenses will be reported during a particular accounting period. The IRS will accept any accounting method that accurately reflects your income and expenses for the year. The *cash method* and the *accrual method* are the two basic accounting methods.

Cash Method The cash method is used by most individuals and small businesses. It is also the accounting method used by most artists and illustrators, and it will likely be your choice, too—unless a substantial part of your income comes from inventory sales.

Using the cash method, you record income when you receive it or when a gallery or agent receives it for you. Similarly, you record expenses when you pay them. Expenses paid in advance are deducted in the year in which they are paid. If expenses are paid in advance for more than one year, they are deducted proportionately in each of those years.

Example

Elaine is an artist using a calendar-year accounting period and the cash accounting method. On August 11, she is paid $1,000 for one of her paintings. When the time comes to file her taxes, she will report the income on her tax return for that calendar year.

Nothing could be simpler, right? However, sometimes income not yet in your possession is taxable. If an amount is "constructively" in your possession—that is, if it has been credited to you or has been made available to you before the end of the year—then it should be included in that year's tax return.

Example

Joel is an illustrator using a calendar-year accounting period and the cash accounting method. On December 29, he received a check in the mail as payment for one of his illustrations. Joel was out of town for the holidays and didn't pick up the check until January 3. Although Joel did not personally receive the check until January 3, he will have to report it on his previous year's tax return because it was made available to him on December 29.

The cash method has many advantages. Its simplicity makes it popular with artists who don't have hours to spend each day on their recordkeeping. Another advantage is that you may postpone reporting income by extending your client's time to pay. The cash method, because it is straightforward and less confusing than other accounting methods, is less likely to produce an error.

Accrual Method The accrual method is a little more involved than the cash method. In the accrual method, you report income at the time you earn it instead of when you receive it. You deduct expenses at the time you incur them rather than when you pay them. If you receive an advance before the end of the year but do not perform the service for which you're being paid until the next year, you may postpone reporting the payment until you earn it. If sales from inventory account for a large part of your income, you may be required to use the accrual method for recording those sales. Check with an accountant.

Example

Phyllis is a painter using a calendar-year accounting period and the accrual accounting method. She signs a contract to execute a painting for a large corporation. She begins the painting in September and completes it in December. However, the cor-poration does not send her check until January 21 of the following year. Since Phyllis uses the accrual method, she will have to report the income in the previous year because she earned it then.

Hybrid Method The *hybrid method* is a combination of the cash and accrual methods. For example, an artist who works on commission and makes sales from inventory might benefit by using the cash method for the commission work and the accrual method for inventory sales.

Change of Accounting Method You are free to choose any accounting method you wish. However, once you've made that decision, you may change your accounting method only with the approval of the Internal Revenue Service. In order to request a change of accounting method, you must file Form 3115, Application for Change in Accounting Method, with the Commissioner of the Internal Revenue Service in Washington, D.C., not more than six months after the beginning of the year in which you wish to make the change.

Setting Up Your Books

The next step to good recordkeeping is to devise a system for keeping up with all your business expenses and income. First, establish some method of keeping your business and personal records separate. For example, keep separate records of which telephone expenses are personal and which are business. It's always a good idea to maintain separate checking accounts for your business and personal expenses to avoid confusion.

Then decide which business records to keep. A good general rule is to keep any receipt related to your business. If in doubt, it's safer to keep the receipt; you can always dispose of it at a later date. Make it a habit, whenever possible, to pay by check, because it's the simplest and best way to keep track of your expenses. When you do pay cash, be sure to obtain receipts. Keep all contracts, bank statements, bank deposit slips, sales slips, cash register tapes, invoices, receipts, and canceled checks, as well as all other income and expense records, such as education costs and entertainment expense records.

Here are a few tips for setting up and maintaining an effective recordkeeping system. The first thing you should do is to divide your income and expense records into separate categories. Then divide each into various subheadings. For example, you would keep your records for commission expenses in a separate place from those for your travel expenses. One type of expense often overlooked is time. You should keep records of the amount of time spent on each project in a diary form, journal, or calendar. Time records show you where you are spending the most time and help you make more effective use of your time in the future. If your records are not too extensive, I might suggest that you keep each category in a labeled envelope. For a more involved system, you may find a file cabinet system more effective.

Another suggestion you might find helpful is to keep a separate job file for each commissioned work. This practice not only makes it easier to retrieve records, but it also reduces the possibility of not being able to identify specific sources of income and expenses when it comes time to do your taxes.

Always make an effort to keep your files in chronological order, if possible. Keep your records up to date: maintaining current records is essential to effective tax planning. It doesn't take much neglect for your records to become hopelessly behind.

Which Recordkeeping Systems Should You Use?

A variety of bookkeeping systems is at your disposal. Single-entry bookkeeping systems simply record the flow of income and expenses. You can use them to prepare an income statement without regard to the balance sheet (assets, liability, and net worth). This would be in the form of a journal, which records income and expense on a daily or monthly basis. Each entry in the journal will include the date, amount of the income or expense, and a brief description, such as an invoice number or description of art supplies.

A double-entry bookkeeping system employs both a journal and a ledger, allowing you to prepare both a balance sheet and an income statement. Transactions are first entered in the journal, then are posted to ledger accounts to indicate income, expense, liability, or net worth. The left side of each account is for debits, and the right side is for credits. The total debits must equal the total credits.

Since you will most likely need only a single-entry system, let's take a look at some journals you might want to use. You can use them in almost any combination, but I've listed them the way they're most often used.

Cash Receipts/Disbursement This is a good system to use if you employ the cash method of accounting. In this system, you maintain two journals (or two sections of the same journal)—one for receipts, one for disbursements.

The *receipts journal* would include a listing for each project showing the client, the amount of invoice, the date the project was completed, and the delivery date. The entry would be listed when payment is received. Daily or monthly summaries can be kept, but the IRS generally looks more favorably on the daily summaries.

The *disbursement journal* would show your monthly paid expenses. You make separate column headings for each of your regular expenses and enter occasional expenses in the miscellaneous column with a notation and the dollar amount. All checks that you write should be entered in this journal.

Accounts Receivable/Payable These journals are commonly used with the accrual method.

In the accounts receivable journal, you should include a listing for each project as it was invoiced, the date the project was completed, delivery date, client, and amount of invoice.

The accounts payable journal is similar to the accounts receivable journal except instead of entering your income, you will enter your expenses. You will list expenses as they are incurred, noting costs such as art supplies, studio expenses, etc. Include such information as quantities, date of bill, and job to which it relates. A later indication of date paid and check number will give you a listing of unpaid expenses.

Other Expense Journals Following are several other ways to keep track of expenses. You can use them in addition to the journals already described in any combination that suits your needs.

Expense Diary: This summary is especially good when receipts are difficult to obtain. The way to use the expense diary is to list the date, payee, purpose of expense, and amount. These expenses can then be summarized and added to your expenses paid by check.

Business Checkbook: As many business expenses as possible should be disbursed through a business checking account. Not only is it a convenient way to pay your bills, but it is also the best way to keep track of your expenses. Don't forget to notate the reason for each check in detail. It's easy to lose track as to why a particular check was written. You should keep any related receipts, sales slips, or other supporting evidence that prove that a particular expense is deductible. If you are audited, a canceled check alone may not be enough supporting evidence for the IRS to allow a disputed deduction. (Remember to keep personal and business checking accounts separate. If the IRS can prove that you intentionally wrote off a personal expense on your business checking account, you could be charged with fraud.)

Petty Cash Vouchers: Any small payments made in cash should be recorded on individual slips. Proof of the transaction should be attached. Ask that the person to whom the payment is made sign the receipt.

Payroll Journal: This journal is used if you have someone on your payroll. A payroll journal assists in the proper withholding and payment of federal, social security, and local taxes from the employee's paycheck.

How Long Should Records Be Kept?

The IRS requires that you keep complete and permanent records, but how long is it necessary to keep past records and tax returns? I would advise that you keep copies of all your past tax returns permanently. The copies of the returns will not take up that much space and may prove invaluable should you be audited or decide to amend a previous year's return.

In most cases, it will be necessary to keep tax records for just four years; however, in some extreme instances, the IRS may ask to review your records as far back as seven years. For instance, if unreported income exceeds 25 percent of your total income for a particular year, then the statute of limitations does not expire for six years. To be safe, you should keep all records at least seven years.

TAXES

Once you've got your books in order, the next challenge is understanding and complying with Federal, state, and local income tax laws. Since state and local laws vary so widely, I won't attempt to address those here. But I will offer some guidance in coping with Federal regulations, including declaring and filing quarterly estimated tax, the rules regarding self-employment tax, and an overview of the most pertinent deductions available to artists.

Estimated Tax

Estimated tax is the method you use to pay tax on income that is not subject to withholding—in general, money you make through being self-employed or freelancing. You will usually make estimated tax payments if you expect to owe more than $500 at year's end and the income tax withheld during the year will be less than both these amounts: (1) 90 percent of the tax shown on that year's tax return; and (2) 100 percent of the tax shown on the previous year's return. Estimated tax payments serve two purposes. They prevent you from owing a large amount of money when you file your return, and they spare you from having to pay an underpayment penalty.

To calculate your estimated tax, you must estimate your adjusted gross income, taxable income, taxes, and credits for the year. Form 1040ES, the form you use to pay estimated tax, provides a worksheet that will assist you in estimating how much to pay.

Estimated tax payments are made in four equal installments. The payments are due on April 15, June 15, September 15, and January 15. (If you use a fiscal year instead of a calendar year, your payment schedule will vary.) If one of those dates falls on a Saturday, Sunday, or holiday, then the due date will be extended to the next business day. If you file your annual tax return on or before February 1 and pay the rest of the money you owe, you don't have to make the January payment. Married couples may pay estimated tax separately or jointly.

If you do not pay enough estimated tax, then you may be liable for the estimated tax penalty, which is figured separately for each quarter. In order to figure the penalty, you will need to complete Form 2210, Underpayment of Estimated Tax by Individuals. It is not necessary to pay the penalty if the total tax on your return minus the amount paid through withholding is less than $500 or if you had no tax liability the previous year.

For more information about estimated tax, refer to IRS Publication 505, Tax Withholding and Estimated Tax.

Estimated Tax Changes Several changes under the 1986 tax law affect estimated tax. The changes affect who will need to make estimated tax payments, the amount of the payments, and the estimated tax penalty.

Beginning in 1988, in order to avoid the estimated tax penalty, you must withhold or make estimated tax payments to cover 90 percent of your current year's tax or 100 percent of your previous year's tax. The penalty rate for underpayment of estimated tax is subject to adjustment every three months instead of every six months.

Self-Employment Tax

If you are an artist in business for yourself, and are not the employee of someone else, you are classified as self-employed. Self-employment income consists of the net profit you made from a profession in which you acted as sole proprietor. To put it simply, you are your own employer and are responsible for paying your social security taxes. Self-employed people pay social security taxes through what is known as the *self-employment tax.* To be liable for self-employment tax, you must have a net self-employment income of $400 or more. The net income is the difference between the self-employment income and your allowable business deductions.

You can be self-employed and still receive a salary from an employer. For example, suppose in 1988 you had a full-time job and earned an annual salary of $20,000. In your spare time, you were a self-employed painter with a net income of $5,000. The social security tax would already be withheld from your salary, but you would still have to pay self-employment tax on the $5,000 you earned as a self-employed artist. However, if you earned a salary of more than $45,000 (the 1988 ceiling), you would not be liable for self-employment tax, no matter how much income you earned as an artist.

Computing Self-Employment Tax You will compute the amount of self-employment tax you owe on Schedule SE, Computation of Social Security Self-Employment Tax. At first glance, the Schedule SE looks complicated, but in most cases, the self-employment tax is easy to compute. Basically all you need to do is multiply your net self-employment income by the self-employment

SCHEDULE SE (Form 1040) Department of the Treasury Internal Revenue Service (3)	**Computation of Social Security Self-Employment Tax** ▶ See Instructions for Schedule SE (Form 1040). ▶ Attach to Form 1040.	OMB No. 1545-0074 1987 Attachment Sequence No. **18**

Name of person with **self-employment** income (as shown on social security card)
TERRY COTTA

Social security number of person with **self-employment** income ▶ 9 8 7 : 6 5 : 4 3 2 1

A If your only self-employment income was from earnings as a minister, member of a religious order, or Christian Science practitioner, AND you filed Form 4361, then DO NOT file Schedule SE. Instead, write "Exempt-Form 4361" on Form 1040, line 48. However, if you filed Form 4361, but have received IRS approval, DO NOT file Schedule SE. Write "Exempt-Form 4029" on Form 1040, line 48. ▶ ☐

B If you filed Form 4029 and have received IRS approval, DO NOT file Schedule SE. Write "Exempt-Form 4029" on Form 1040, line 48.

C If your only earnings subject to self-employment tax are wages from an electing church or church-controlled organization that is exempt from employer social security taxes and you are not a minister or a member of a religious order, skip lines 1–8. Enter zero on line 9. Continue with line 11a.

Part I Regular Computation of Net Earnings From Self-Employment

| 1 | Net farm profit (or loss) from Schedule F (Form 1040), line 37, and farm partnerships, Schedule K-1 (Form 1065), line 14a | 1 | |
| 2 | Net profit (or loss) from Schedule C (Form 1040), line 31, and Schedule K-1 (Form 1065), line 14a (other than farming). (See Instructions for other income to report.) Employees of an electing church or church-controlled organization DO NOT enter your Form W-2 wages on line 2. See the Instructions | 2 | 1 0 0 0 0 |

Part II Optional Computation of Net Earnings From Self-Employment (See "Who Can Use Schedule SE" in the Instructions.)

See Instructions for limitations. Generally, this part may be used **only** if you meet any of the following tests:

A Your **gross farm income**[1] was not more than $2,400; **or**

B Your **gross farm income**[1] was more than $2,400 and your **net farm profits**[2] were **less** than $1,600; **or**

C Your **net nonfarm profits**[3] were less than $1,600 and your **net** nonfarm profits[3] were also **less** than two-thirds (2/3) of your **gross** nonfarm income.[4]

Note: If line 2 above is two-thirds (2/3) or more of your gross nonfarm income[4], or, if line 2 is $1,600 or more, you may **not** use the optional method.
[1]From Schedule F (Form 1040), line 12, and Schedule K-1 (Form 1065), line 14b.   [3]From Schedule C (Form 1040), line 31, and Schedule K-1 (Form 1065), line 14a.
[2]From Schedule F (Form 1040), line 37, and Schedule K-1 (Form 1065), line 14a.   [4]From Schedule C (Form 1040), line 5, and Schedule K-1 (Form 1065), line 14c.

3	Maximum income for optional methods	3	$1,600	00
4	Farm Optional Method—If you meet test A or B above, enter the **smaller of:** two-thirds (2/3) of gross farm income from Schedule F (Form 1040), line 12, and farm partnerships, Schedule K-1 (Form 1065), line 14b; **or** $1,600	4		
5	Subtract line 4 from line 3	5		
6	Nonfarm Optional Method—If you meet test C above, enter the **smallest of:** two-thirds (2/3) of gross nonfarm income from Schedule C (Form 1040), line 5, and Schedule K-1 (Form 1065), line 14c (other than farming); **or** $1,600; **or,** if you elected the farm optional method, the amount on line 5 ▶	6		

Part III Computation of Social Security Self-Employment Tax

7	Enter the amount from Part I, line 1, **or,** if you elected the farm optional method, Part II, line 4	7		
8	Enter the amount from Part I, line 2, **or,** if you elected the nonfarm optional method, Part II, line 6	8	1 0 0 0 0	
9	Add lines 7 and 8. If less than $400, do not file this schedule. (Exception: If you are an employee of an electing church or church-controlled organization and the total of lines 7 and 8 is less than $400, enter zero and complete the rest of this schedule.)	9	1 0 0 0 0	
10	The largest amount of combined wages and self-employment earnings subject to social security or railroad retirement tax (tier 1) for 1987 is	10	$43,800	00
11a	Total social security wages and tips from Forms W-2 and railroad retirement compensation (tier 1). **Note:** Medicare qualified government employees whose wages are only subject to the 1.45% medicare (hospital insurance benefits) tax and employees of certain church or church-controlled organizations should **not** include those wages on this line. (See Instructions.) 11a			
b	Unreported tips subject to social security tax from Form 4137, line 9, or to railroad retirement tax (tier 1) 11b			
c	Add lines 11a and 11b	11c		
12a	Subtract line 11c from line 10. (If zero or less, enter zero.)	12a	1 0 0 0 0	
b	Enter your medicare qualified government wages if you are required to use the worksheet in Part III of the Instructions. 12b			
c	Enter your Form W-2 wages of $100 or more from an electing church or church-controlled organization. 12c			
d	Add lines 9 and 12c	12d		
13	Enter the smaller of line 12a or line 12d	13	1 0 0 0 0	
	If line 13 is $43,800, enter $5,387.40 on line 14. Otherwise, multiply line 13 by .123 and enter the result on line 14		×.123	
14	Self-employment tax. Enter this amount on Form 1040, line 48	14	1 2 3 0	

For Paperwork Reduction Act Notice, see Form 1040 Instructions.   Schedule SE (Form 1040) 1987 tax rate. For example, if your net self-employment income was $10,000 in 1987, you would multiply this figure by the self-employment tax rate of 12.3 percent and arrive at a self-employment tax for the year of $1,230. This amount would be computed on your Schedule SE and brought over to line 48 of your Form 1040, self-employment tax, and added in with your other taxes.

If you follow the Schedule SE line by line, the computation of your self-employment tax will be no problem, even if you have additional salaried income. If you file a joint return and your spouse also has self-employment income, he or she must file a separate Schedule SE to compute his or her self-employment tax. Filing two separate Schedule SEs insures that each taxpayer receives proper credit for their contributions to the social security program. Following is an example of a completed Schedule SE.

The bad news about the self-employment tax is that it is much higher than the FICA tax withheld from the paychecks of salaried employees. In 1987, the FICA tax rate was 7.15 percent; it increased to 7.51 percent in 1988. On the other hand, the self-employment tax rate was 12.3 percent in 1987, and it rose to 13.02 percent in 1988. (These figures do not include a 2 percent credit, which will be eliminated in 1989.) The reason the self-employment tax is so much higher than the regular FICA tax is that the employer of a salaried employee is required to match the employee's FICA contribution. As a self-employed person, you are both employer and employee, so you must pay both the employer's and the employee's contributions to FICA. The good news is that, unlike the salaried employee, you can deduct allowable business expenses to reduce both your self-employment and regular taxes.

Self-Employment Tax Increases As you are aware, the social security taxes are constantly rising, and so is the self-employment tax. The self-employment tax rate was 12.3 percent in 1987; it rose to 13.02 percent in 1988. After 1989, the 2 percent credit will be repealed. What's more, the income base,

the amount subject to the tax, has increased every year since 1971. In 1987, the income cutoff was $43,800; in 1988, it went up to $45,000.

Deductions

Legitimate business deductions are by far the best way you can lower the amount of income tax you owe. However, it can be quite a job to keep up with what is and what is not deductible—and the IRS places the burden of proof on you in the event any of your deductions are challenged.

The task of understanding deductions was further complicated by the extensive changes under the new law. For instance, a taxpayer taking the home office deduction may no longer have a net loss resulting from the deduction. Also, travel and entertainment expenses are no longer fully deductible. There have also been significant changes in educational expenses, prizes and awards, and depreciation.

After reading this section, you will know which deductions you may take and which you may not.

The Home Office Deduction

It's very common for an artist to have a studio in his or her home. You'll have obvious advantages with this type of arrangement. You can work whenever you're inspired without having to commute crosstown to your studio.

Having a studio in your home will bring you financial advantages as well. One of the biggest advantages is not having to rent another office. Renting a studio can be a major expense for an artist. In addition, the home office deduction can be a big tax break for an artist. With a home office, you can use Schedule A to deduct the business portion of expenses, such as mortgage interest, real estate taxes, auto expenses, office supplies, rent, maintenance, utilities, and insurance. (Note, however, that these expenses are deductible only to the extent that they exceed 2 percent of your adjusted gross income.)

You should also be warned that the IRS is

not known for giving taxpayers a break without stipulations, and this deduction is no exception. You must meet three criteria before you can qualify for the home office deduction: exclusive use, regular use, and use as your principal place of business.

Exclusive Use To satisfy this requirement, the home office must be used exclusively for your business activity. The old saying that business and pleasure don't mix was never truer than in this situation. Once you designate an area to be your office, you may no longer use it for your personal benefit. For example, your recreation room cannot double as an office.

In recent years, this distinction has been repeatedly challenged in the courts, and the rules governing the barriers between personal and business use have become more lenient. Recent court rulings have declared that you may use a room for both an office and for personal use only if you clearly divide the space into separate areas. However, considering the stringent requirements that the IRS places on the home office deduction, it would be in your best interest never to use space set aside for an office for personal use.

Regular Use The space set aside for your office must also be used on a regular basis. The IRS doesn't offer any specific guidelines on what constitutes regular use, so it's a matter of interpretation. If you use your office a given number of hours a week, then that might indicate a regular schedule. The use of an office on a regular basis means that it is used continually and frequently and not occasionally or incidentally.

Principal Place of Business Your home office must also be your principal place of business. It should be the place where you meet with clients during the normal course of business. You may have more than one business location and still take the home office deduction so long as you can support that your home office is your principal place of business. Factors to consider in determining whether your home office is your

principal place of business include:

1. The amount of time you spend working in the office.
2. The amount of income you derive from doing business there.
3. The type of facilities you have installed that relate to your business activity.

Some artists have another business that generates more income than they derive from the sale of their art. For example, you may have a full-time job for which you have an office at another location. You can still take your home office deduction as long as it's your principal place of business for your secondary source of income, in this case your income as an artist. In the past, the IRS has challenged this interpretation in the courts, but so far, it has been unsuccessful.

However, if you are a professional artist working for someone else in that capacity with no self-employment income, it is decidedly more difficult to qualify for the home office deduction. According to IRS regulations, a person in this situation must use his home office for the "convenience of the employer." This means that if the employer provides an office for you elsewhere, you cannot deduct your home office.

Separate Structures If you have a work space adjoining your residence, the requirements for qualifying as a home office deduction are not as stringent. This separate structure may be a garage, a small, freestanding building, etc. The separate structure still must meet the regular-use and exclusive-use requirements, but it does not have to be your principal place of business. It must, however, be used only in connection with your business activity.

Storage of Inventory The storage of inventory is one of the exceptions to the exclusive-use test. You may be allowed to deduct expenses relating to using part of your home for the storage of inventory, even if the use is not exclusive. The inventory may consist of your artwork, supplies, and other art-related materials. In order to claim this deduction, you must first meet the following five requirements:

1. The inventory must be used in your business.
2. Your business must be the wholesale or retailing of a product.
3. Your home must be the sole fixed location of your business.
4. The storage space must be used on a regular basis.
5. The space must be a separately identifiable area suitable for storage.

The Tax Advantages of Having an Office Located in Your Home

Having a home office deduction provides you with many tax advantages. You can deduct many items that would not otherwise be deductible, such as a portion of your rent, property taxes, gas and electric bills, water, depreciation, mortgage interest, home insurance, repairs, etc.

You may not only depreciate a portion of your home used for business, but also the furniture and equipment used in your office. However, these costs must be deducted according to a depreciation schedule. *Depreciation* is a method by which a capital asset (building or equipment) is expensed over a number of years. For example, furniture and fixtures may be depreciated over a seven-year period, while the recovery period for a building or office is 31½ years.

Remember that you cannot depreciate items that benefit only the part of the house devoted to personal use. Direct expenses, those relating to the office, are fully deductible. An example of a direct expense would be painting the office. Indirect expenses, those relating to both the business and personal use of the house, are only partially deductible.

Figuring the Business Percentage To figure the percentage of your home expenses that is deductible, you should divide the square footage of your office space by the total square footage of your home. (To determine the square footage of a room, multiply the length of the room by the width.) This percentage of your expenses is deductible.

Example
Raymond has an office in his home that measures 200 square feet. His home measures 2,000 square feet. Therefore, his business percentage would be 200 divided by 2,000, or 10 percent. If he had $5,000 in expenses, then 10 percent of those expenses, or $500, would be deductible.

If calculating your office space in this method is too complicated, then you may use a simpler method to determine your business percentage. If your office is roughly the same size as the other rooms in your house, then you may figure the business percentage by dividing the number of rooms used for office space (usually this will be *one*) by the number of rooms in your house.

Example
Marie uses one room of her house for an office. She has ten rooms in her house. The business percentage would be 1 divided by 10 or 10 percent. If Marie had expenses of $10,000, she could deduct 10 percent of that total, or $1,000.

If you rent rather than own a home, you may deduct the appropriate percentage of the rent you pay. For example, if you have five rooms in your apartment and you use one of them as an office, then you may deduct one-fifth, or 20 percent, of the rent. If you paid $500 a month rent, then 20 percent, or $100, would be deductible.

Deduction Limitation Your total office deduction for the business use of your home cannot exceed the gross income that you derive from its business use. To put it simply, you cannot take a net business loss resulting from a home office deduction.

If the result is a net loss, then you must deduct your expenses in the following order:

1. Direct business expenses, such as supplies necessary to run your business,

auto expenses, cost of goods sold, etc.
2. Mortgage interest, property taxes, and casualty losses.
3. Operating expenses, such as utilities, insurance, etc.
4. Depreciation.

When you have reached the point on this schedule where deductions equal gross income, you can claim no more deductions for that year. However, you can carry over the remaining expenses to be deducted in future years.

Example
Roger is an illustrator with a gross income of $6,000. He figured that his allowable home office deduction was $7,000. He had direct business expenses of $3,000, mortgage interest and real estate taxes of $2,000, operating expenses of $1,000, and depreciation of $1,000. He would be able to deduct his direct business expenses, mortgage interest, real estate taxes, and operating expenses because these expenses total $6,000, which equals his gross income. However, since he cannot take a loss, he would have to carry forward the $1,000 depreciation deduction to another year.

Recordkeeping Because the home office deduction is closely scrutinized by the IRS, proper recordkeeping is essential as a safeguard in the event this deduction is challenged. I recommend that you keep a log book of business activities taking place in your home office. Include such information as the dates and times the office was in use, any business transacted, the names of the clients visiting your office and what business was discussed, all sales transacted, etc. You need to keep a detailed record of all income and expenses, copies of all receipts, canceled checks, and all other records of your expenditures. The IRS insists that your home office records substantiate all the following:

1. The part of the home used for business purposes.

2. That the office is used exclusively and regularly for business as either your principal place of business or as the location where you meet with clients during the normal course of business.
3. The amount of expenses related to your home office.

The Drawbacks of the Home Office Deduction
We've examined the many advantages of the home office deduction; let's consider the drawbacks as well. The principal drawback is that you greatly increase your chances of being audited when you take the home office deduction. For this reason, you must be certain of every deduction you take and have the records to back them up. The burden of proof is on you, and the IRS frequently disallows the home office deduction.

Also be aware that if you sell your home in the same year that you claim a home office, you will not be able to postpone paying taxes on the gain from the sale. Any profit you realize from the office portion of your home must be claimed as ordinary income. If you know ahead of time that you're going to be selling your house, then it would be beneficial to stop deducting your home office expenses a year before the sale.

You may wish to refer to IRS Publication 587, Business Use of Your Home, for additional information about the home office deduction.

Changes in the Home Office Deduction
As previously mentioned, you can no longer use your home office deduction to produce a net loss on your business schedule. The deduction is now permitted only if it does not exceed your net profit from the sale of your artwork. Deductions in excess of the limit may be carried forward to later years, when the same limitations will apply.

If you are depreciating a studio at home for the first time, then you will have to use $31\frac{1}{2}$ years as a life instead of 19 years, because the recovery period of commercial property has been extended.

Other Schedule A Deductions

Miscellaneous deductions (including the home office deduction) are reported on Schedule A. These deductions, which under the old law were fully deductible, are now deductible only to the extent that the total amount of the miscellaneous itemized deductions exceeds 2 percent of your adjusted gross income. Schedule A deductions include professional society dues, professional books, magazines, journals, periodicals. employment related education, union dues, work clothes, 80 percent of unreimbursed employee business-related entertainment and meal expenses, work-related supplies, home office expenses, tax and investment counsel fees, expenses incurred searching for employment, safe deposit box rental, and certain other unreimbursed employee business expenses. If you file a Schedule C as a self-employed individual, these expenses are deductible against reported income unless otherwise limited (i.e., meals and entertainment).

Schedule C Deductions

For the self-employed taxpayer, Schedule C can be the most important schedule on the return. Schedule C is where you will report your self-employment income and, best of all, claim your business deductions. As a self-employed artist, using Schedule C properly can reduce your taxes significantly.

You will report any income from which there has been no tax withheld on Schedule C, Profit or Loss From Business or Profession. You can also reduce your gross self-employment income directly by claiming allowable business-related deductions on Schedule C. Some of the most common deductible expenses for an artist, such as canvas, paint, framing, model fees, and agents, are included in Schedule C deductions.

Since Schedule C is so important and since you must complete Schedule C if you are self employed, let's work our way through this form step by step.

In the entity portion, you will fill out your name and social security number. Your business address will be the address of your studio or office. The next section of Schedule C asks a series of questions about your business practices. You will have to indicate whether you use a cash or accrual accounting method. You must also indicate if you deduct expenses for an office in your home.

Part I of Schedule C is devoted to income. In this section, you will report your gross sales or receipts. You will also subtract costs of goods sold, if any. (You can compute the costs of goods sold on Part III of Schedule C.) Using the computation in Part I, you will arrive at your gross income.

Part II of Schedule C is for claiming business deductions. For a business expense to be deductible, it must be "ordinary and necessary" for conducting your profession. What expenses qualify as ordinary and necessary is a matter of interpretation. My advice is that if you can't support the expense with some kind of documentation, then don't claim it. It must be an expense relating to your line of work and not a personal expense.

Allowable deductions come under a variety of headings. You would be wise to keep separate records under each heading, not only because it makes it easier to report on your Schedule C, but also in the event any of these deductions are questioned by the IRS during an audit. For more information, refer to the section of this book on record-keeping.

Here are some of the most common allowable expenses for an artist, listed under the appropriate headings on Schedule C.

Advertising: On this line, you may deduct any advertising expenses, such as slides, portfolios, printing costs of brochures, business cards, resumes, etc.

Commissions: List here any commissions paid to galleries, agents, or art representatives.

Dues and Publications: Deductibles include art books and magazines, as well as union and membership dues.

Insurance: Insurance on art in transit or work being exhibited, fire, theft, and liabili-

SCHEDULE C (Form 1040)	**Profit or (Loss) From Business or Profession**	OMB No. 1545-0074

SCHEDULE C
(Form 1040)

Department of the Treasury
Internal Revenue Service (3)

Profit or (Loss) From Business or Profession
(Sole Proprietorship)
Partnerships, Joint Ventures, etc., Must File Form 1065.
▶ Attach to Form 1040, Form 1041, or Form 1041S.   ▶ See Instructions for Schedule C (Form 1040).

OMB No. 1545-0074

1987

Attachment
Sequence No. **09**

Name of proprietor	Social security number (SSN)
TERRY COTTA	987 65 4321

A Principal business or profession, including product or service (see Instructions)

ARTIST

B Principal business code
(from Part IV) ▶ 8 8 8 8

C Business name and address ▶ 11275 BRIDGETOWN RD, CINCINNATI, OH 45267

D Employer ID number (Not SSN)

E Method(s) used to value closing inventory:

(1) ☒ Cost   **(2)** ☐ Lower of cost or market   **(3)** ☐ Other (attach explanation)

F Accounting method: **(1)** ☒ Cash   **(2)** ☐ Accrual   **(3)** ☐ Other (specify) ▶ ....

		Yes	No
G	Was there any change in determining quantities, costs, or valuations between opening and closing inventory? (If "Yes," attach explanation.)		☒
H	Are you deducting expenses for an office in your home?	☒	
I	Did you file **Form 941** for this business for any quarter in 1987?		☒
J	Did you "materially participate" in the operation of this business during 1987? (If "No," see Instructions for limitations on losses.)	☒	
K	Was this business in operation at the end of 1987?	☒	
L	How many months was this business in operation during 1987? ▶		

M If this schedule includes a loss, credit, deduction, income, or other tax benefit relating to a tax shelter required to be registered, check here. ▶ ☐
If you check this box, you **MUST** attach **Form 8271**.

Part I Income

1a Gross receipts or sales		1a	11 000
b Less: Returns and allowances		1b	
c Subtract line 1b from line 1a and enter the balance here		1c	11 000
2 Cost of goods sold and/or operations (from Part III, line 8)		2	
3 Subtract line 2 from line 1c and enter the **gross profit** here		3	11 000
4 Other income (including windfall profit tax credit or refund received in 1987).		4	
5 Add lines 3 and 4. This is the **gross income** ▶		5	11 000

Part II Deductions

6 Advertising	50	
7 Bad debts from sales or services (see Instructions.)		
8 Bank service charges		
9 Car and truck expenses		
10 Commissions	150	
11 Depletion		
12 Depreciation and section 179 deduction from Form 4562 (not included in Part III)		
13 Dues and publications	200	
14 Employee benefit programs		
15 Freight (not included in Part III)		
16 Insurance	100	
17 Interest:		
a Mortgage (paid to financial institutions)		
b Other		
18 Laundry and cleaning	50	
19 Legal and professional services	250	
20 Office expense	50	
21 Pension and profit-sharing plans		
22 Rent on business property		

23 Repairs		
24 Supplies (not included in Part III)		
25 Taxes		
26 Travel, meals, and entertainment:		
a Travel		150
b Total meals and entertainment		
c Enter 20% of line 26b subject to limitations (see Instructions)		
d Subtract line 26c from 26b		
27 Utilities and telephone		
28a Wages		
b Jobs credit		
c Subtract line 28b from 28a		
29 Other expenses (list type and amount):		
....		
....		
....		
....		
....		

30 Add amounts in columns for lines 6 through 29. These are the **total deductions** ▶		30	1000
31 **Net profit or (loss).** Subtract line 30 from line 5. If a profit, enter here and on Form 1040, line 13, and on Schedule SE, line 2 (or line 5 of Form 1041 or Form 1041S). If a loss, you **MUST** go on to line 32		31	10000

32 If you have a loss, you **MUST** answer this question: "Do you have amounts for which you are not at risk in this business?" (See Instructions.) ☐ Yes ☐ No
If "Yes," you **MUST** attach **Form 6198**. If "No," enter the loss on Form 1040, line 13, and on Schedule SE, line 2 (or line 5 of Form 1041 or Form 1041S).

For Paperwork Reduction Act Notice, see Form 1040 Instructions.

Schedule C (Form 1040) 1987

Schedule C (Form 1040) 1987   Page **2**

Part III   Cost of Goods Sold and/or Operations (See Schedule C Instructions for Part III)

1	Inventory at beginning of year. (If different from last year's closing inventory, attach explanation.)	1
2	Purchases less cost of items withdrawn for personal use	2
3	Cost of labor. (Do not include salary paid to yourself.)	3
4	Materials and supplies	4
5	Other costs	5
6	Add lines 1 through 5	6
7	Less: Inventory at end of year	7
8	**Cost of goods sold and/or operations.** Subtract line 7 from line 6. Enter here and in Part I, line 2	8

Part IV   Codes for Principal Business or Professional Activity

Locate the major business category that best describes your activity (for example, Retail Trade, Services, etc.). Within the major category, select the activity code that identifies (or most closely identifies) the business or profession that is the principal source of your sales or receipts. **Enter this 4-digit code on line B on page 1 of Schedule C. (Note:** *If your principal source of income is from farming activities, you should file* **Schedule F** *(Form 1040), Farm Income and Expenses.)*

Construction

Code

0018   Operative builders (building for own account)

General contractors

0034   Residential building
0059   Nonresidential building
0075   Highway and street construction
3889   Other heavy construction (pipe laying, bridge construction, etc.)

Building trade contractors, including repairs

0232   Plumbing, heating, air conditioning
0257   Painting and paper hanging
0273   Electrical work
0299   Masonry, dry wall, stone, tile
0414   Carpentering and flooring
0430   Roofing, siding, and sheet metal
0455   Concrete work
0471   Water well drilling
0885   Other building trade contractors (excavation, glazing, etc.)

Manufacturing, Including Printing and Publishing

0612   Bakeries selling at retail
0638   Other food products and beverages
0653   Textile mill products
0679   Apparel and other textile products
0695   Leather, footware, handbags, etc.
0810   Furniture and fixtures
0836   Lumber and other wood products
0851   Printing and publishing
0877   Paper and allied products
0893   Chemicals and allied products
1016   Rubber and plastics products
1032   Stone, clay, and glass products
1057   Primary metal industries
1073   Fabricated metal products
1099   Machinery and machine shops
1115   Electric and electronic equipment
1313   Transportation equipment
1339   Instruments and related products
1883   Other manufacturing industries

Mining and Mineral Extraction

1511   Metal mining
1537   Coal mining
1552   Oil and gas
1719   Quarrying and nonmetallic mining

Agricultural Services, Forestry, and Fishing

1917   Soil preparation services
1933   Crop services
1958   Veterinary services, including pets
1974   Livestock breeding
1990   Other animal services
2113   Farm labor and management services
2212   Horticulture and landscaping
2238   Forestry, except logging
0836   Logging
2279   Fishing, hunting, and trapping

Wholesale Trade—Selling Goods to Other Businesses, Government, or Institutions, etc.

Durable goods, including machinery, equipment, wood, metals, etc.

2618   Selling for your own account

Code

2634   Agent or broker for other firms—more than 50% of gross sales on commission

Nondurable goods, including food, fiber, chemicals, etc.

2659   Selling for your own account
2675   Agent or broker for other firms—more than 50% of gross sales on commission

Retail Trade—Selling Goods to Individuals and Households

3012   Selling door-to-door, by telephone or party plan, or from mobile unit
3038   Catalog or mail order
3053   Vending machine selling

Selling From Store, Showroom, or Other Fixed Location

Food, beverages, and drugs

3079   Eating places (meals or snacks)
3095   Drinking places (alcoholic beverages)
3210   Grocery stores (general line)
0612   Bakeries selling at retail
3236   Other food stores (meat, produce, candy, etc.)
3251   Liquor stores
3277   Drug stores

Automotive and service stations

3319   New car dealers (franchised)
3335   Used car dealers
3517   Other automotive dealers (motorcycles, recreational vehicles, etc.)
3533   Tires, accessories, and parts
3558   Gasoline service stations

General merchandise, apparel, and furniture

3715   Variety stores
3731   Other general merchandise stores
3756   Shoe stores
3772   Men's and boys' clothing stores
3913   Women's ready-to-wear stores
3921   Women's accessory and specialty stores and furriers
3939   Family clothing stores
3954   Other apparel and accessory stores
3970   Furniture stores
3996   TV, audio, and electronics
3988   Computer and software stores
4119   Household appliance stores
4317   Other home furnishing stores (china, floor coverings, drapes, etc.)
4333   Music and record stores

Building, hardware, and garden supply

4416   Building materials dealers
4432   Paint, glass, and wallpaper stores
4457   Hardware stores
4473   Nurseries and garden supply stores

Other retail stores

4614   Used merchandise and antique stores (except used motor vehicle parts)
4630   Gift, novelty, and souvenir shops
4655   Florists
4671   Jewelry stores

Code

4697   Sporting goods and bicycle shops
4812   Boat dealers
4838   Hobby, toy, and game shops
4853   Camera and photo supply stores
4879   Optical goods stores
4895   Luggage and leather goods stores
5017   Book stores, excluding newsstands
5033   Stationery stores
5058   Fabric and needlework stores
5074   Mobile home dealers
5090   Fuel dealers (except gasoline)
5884   Other retail stores

Real Estate, Insurance, Finance, and Related Services

5512   Real estate agents and managers
5538   Operators and lessors of buildings (except developers)
5553   Operators and lessors of other real property (except developers)
5710   Subdividers and developers, except cemeteries
5736   Insurance agents and services
5751   Security and commodity brokers, dealers, and investment services
5777   Other real estate, insurance, and financial activities

Transportation, Communications, Public Utilities, and Related Services

6114   Taxicabs
6312   Bus and limousine transportation
6338   Trucking (except trash collection)
6510   Trash collection without own dump
6536   Public warehousing
6551   Water transportation
6619   Air transportation
6635   Travel agents and tour operators
6650   Other transportation and related services
6676   Communication services
6692   Utilities, including dumps, snowplowing, road cleaning, etc.

Services (Providing Personal, Professional, and Business Services)

Hotels and other lodging places

7096   Hotels, motels, and tourist homes
7211   Rooming and boarding houses
7237   Camps and camping parks

Laundry and cleaning services

7419   Coin-operated laundries and dry cleaning
7435   Other laundry, dry cleaning, and garment services
7450   Carpet and upholstery cleaning
7476   Janitorial and related services (building, house, and window cleaning)

Business and/or personal services

7617   Legal services (or lawyer)
7633   Income tax preparation
7658   Accounting and bookkeeping
7674   Engineering, surveying, and architectural

Code

7690   Management, consulting, and public relations
7716   Advertising, except direct mail
7732   Employment agencies and personnel supply
7757   Computer and data processing, including repair and leasing
7773   Equipment rental and leasing (except computer or automotive)
7914   Investigative and protective services
7880   Other business services

Personal services

8110   Beauty shops (or beautician)
8318   Barber shop (or barber)
8334   Photographic portrait studios
8516   Shoe repair and shine services
8532   Funeral services and crematories
8714   Child day care
8730   Teaching or tutoring
8755   Counseling (except health practitioners)
8771   Ministers and chaplains
6882   Other personal services

Automotive services

8813   Automotive rental or leasing, without driver
8839   Parking, except valet
8854   General automotive repairs
8870   Specialized automotive repairs (brake, body repairs, paint, etc.)
8896   Other automotive services (wash, towing, etc.)

Miscellaneous repair, except computers

9019   TV and audio equipment repair
9035   Other electrical equipment repair
9050   Reupholstery and furniture repair
2881   Other equipment repair

Medical and health services

9217   Offices and clinics of medical doctors (MD's)
9233   Offices and clinics of dentists
9258   Osteopathic physicians and surgeons
9274   Chiropractors
9290   Optometrists
9415   Registered and practical nurses
9431   Other licensed health practitioners
9456   Dental laboratories
9472   Nursing and personal care facilities
9886   Other health services

Amusement and recreational services

8557   Physical fitness facilities
9613   Videotape rental stores
9639   Motion picture theaters
9654   Other motion picture and TV film and tape activities
9670   Bowling alleys
9696   Professional sports and racing, including promoters and managers
9811   Theatrical performers, musicians, agents, producers, and related services
9837   Other amusement and recreational services

8888   Unable to classify

ty insurance, etc.

Laundry and Cleaning: The cleaning of clothing used while painting in addition to costs incurred by the cleaning of your studio.

Legal and Professional Services: Fees paid to appraisers, attorneys, accountants, etc., in connection with your profession.

Office Expenses: Office expenses not listed elsewhere, such as framing, or postage.

Travel, Meals, and Entertainment: All travel and entertainment expenses, including meals, lodging, transportation, etc. Meals and entertainment expenses are now only 80 percent deductible. (See below for a more detailed discussion of these expenses.)

Other Expenses: List any jury fees, gallery opening expenses, entry fees, workshop expenses, etc.

If both you and your spouse are self employed, you should file separate Schedule Cs. Following is an example of a completed Schedule C.

Entertainment, Meals, and Travel Expenses Business meals and entertainment may be deducted only if business is discussed before, during, or after the meal. You must be able to prove that the expenses are directly related to the active conduct of your business. Under the new tax laws, only 80 percent of these expenses may be deducted, Uncle Sam's way of turning the three-martini lunch into a two-martini lunch. While this change was put into effect to discourage business people from taking excessive business lunches, it will also affect artists who entertain potential clients. The 80 percent limitation also applies to meals away from home for business purposes, but it does not apply to travel and lodging expenses.

Also, the IRS is planning to crack down on extravagant meal expenses, so if you're planning to impress clients by taking them to a five-star restaurant, be prepared to pay it out of your own pocket. You are not required to keep a receipt for entertainment expenses of twenty-five dollars or less, but it would be a good policy to keep all business-related receipts.

To be deductible, travel expenses must qualify as ordinary and necessary expenses incurred while traveling away from home overnight. Deductible travel expenses include air, rail, and bus fares, the cost of operating an automobile, taxi fares, lodging, telephone and telegraph expenses, and other similar travel-related expenses. Travel expenses are allowed for attending a convention or seminar only if it relates directly to your business or trade.

It is essential that you keep complete and accurate records of your travel and entertainment expenses. Records you keep to support your travel expenses should include an entry for every amount spent on the trip (keep all receipts), the dates of the trip, the destination of your travel, and the business purpose of the trip. For your entertainment expenses, also keep a record of each expenditure, the date the entertainment took place, the location of the entertainment, the purpose of the entertainment, and the names of persons entertained.

For additional information, you may wish to consult IRS Publication 463, Travel, Entertainment, and Gift Expenses.

The Tax Reform Act and How it Affects You
The Tax Reform Act of 1986 is the most sweeping revision of the tax code in more than forty years. It will affect virtually every taxpayer. The main purpose of the Tax Reform Act was to simplify taxes and lower the tax rates for most individual taxpayers. However, the scope of the changes makes it imperative that you understand the new tax laws in order to fully take advantage of them. The changes in the new tax laws are too numerous and complex to completely explain in the space provided, so I have summarized the major changes, highlighting the ones most likely to affect you as an artist.

Deduction of Art Materials Probably no change under the new tax laws has a more adverse effect on artists than the change in the way the cost of art materials is deducted. Under the old rules, art-related expenses were deducted in the year in which they were incurred. For example, if you incurred expenses in 1984, then you deducted the full amount of those expenses on your 1984 tax return.

Under the provisions imposed under the Tax Reform Act of 1986 artists would only have been able to deduct expenses on works sold during the year. This meant that, if an artist incurred expenses on a project that produced no income, expenses couldn't be deducted in that year. Another detrimental effect of the provision was that these deductions had to be spread out over the income life of the project. This meant that, if you finished a work which earned income over a number of years, you would have to estimate how many years revenue would be generated and spread out your deductions over that period.

Lobbyists for artists protested these changes and the Internal Revenue Service, realizing the inequities of the new rules, proposed a compromise plan. Art-related expenses may now be deducted using a new three-year method. Under the new proposal 50 percent of all art related expenses may be deducted in the first year, 25 percent in the second year, and the remaining 25 percent in the third year, regardless of when income is realized. The concession has not satisfied many artists, who continue to lobby insisting that the pre-1986 Tax Reform Act rules for deducting art-related expenses be restored. At the time of this writing, the three-year method was in effect. However, pending legislation could change the law at any time.

Educational Income and Expenses Only a candidate for a degree may exclude amounts received as a qualified scholarship from his or her income. A qualified scholarship is any amount received for tuitions and fees, books, and supplies required for courses. Scholarships for room, board, and travel expenses must be counted as income.

Payments for services such as teaching and research grants must be included as income, even if the services are a condition of receiving the grant.

The expenses of attending conferences or educational programs are deductible only if "no significant amount of personal pleasure" is derived. Travel done solely for educational value is not deductible unless it is necessary to travel to do research or attend courses, i.e., the research materials or courses are not available in one's home town.

Depreciation The Tax Reform Act of 1986 resulted in major changes in the way depreciation is figured. Depreciation on art equipment is taken over five years, but under the new law, it will compute at a faster rate. If you purchase furniture for your office or studio, you can not depreciate it over seven years. Under the old law, it was depreciated over five years.

Prizes and Awards All prizes and awards earned after 1986 are completely taxable. Prior to the new laws' going into effect, certain awards for artistic achievement had a tax-free status. The only exception to the rule is if you donate 100 percent of your prize or award to a charitable organization.

Health Insurance After January 1, 1987, self-employed persons may deduct 25 percent of any health-insurance-plan expenses. It is taken on line 25 of Form 1040 as an adjustment to income. The deduction may not exceed your net self-employment earnings.

Changes to Itemized Deductions The new law brought many changes to the deductions itemized on Schedule A. Here are a few highlights.

Mortgage Interest: Previously, mortgage interest was fully deductible, but now the deduction is limited for certain interest.

Other Personal Interest: Personal interest, such as credit card interest and interest on new car loans, used to be fully deductible, but the deduction is being phased out over a four-year-period. After 1990, these items can't be deducted at all.

State and Local Sales Taxes: The state and local sales taxes, once fully deductible under the old law, are not deductible after 1986.

Medical Expenses: Medical expenses are deductible to the extent they exceed 7.5 percent of your adjusted gross income. For tax years 1986 and before, medical expenses were deductible to the extent they exceeded 5 percent of the adjusted gross income.

Charitable Contributions: After 1986, charitable contributions are deductible only as an itemized deduction. They were previously deductible for both itemizers and non-itemizers.

Moving Expenses: Moving expenses are now deductible only as an itemized deduction. Previously, these expenses were deductible as an adjustment to income.

The Tax Brackets One of the changes that will affect every taxpayer are the new tax rates. The changes should result in lower taxes for most taxpayers. The old system included fifteen separate tax brackets ranging from 0 to 50 percent. There are now only two tax-rate brackets, 15 percent and 28 percent. Taxpayers within certain higher income ranges are also subject to a 5 percent surcharge on taxable income. The income brackets are indexed so that inflation will not result in a tax increase.

1988 TAX BRACKETS

Married Filing Jointly or Qualifying Widow(er)

Over	Taxable income But not over	Tax rate
$0	$29,750	15%
$29,750 up		28%

Single

Over	Taxable income But not over	Tax rate
$0	$17,850	15%
$17,850 up		28%

Married Filing Separately

Over	Taxable income But not over	Tax rate
$0	$14,875	15%
$14,875 up		28%

Head of Household

Over	Taxable income But not over	Tax rate
$0	$23,900	15%
$23,900 up		28%

Beginning in 1988, taxpayers within the following income ranges will be subject to an additional 5 percent tax to phase out the benefit of the 15 percent tax rate.

INCOME SUBJECT TO ADDITIONAL 5% TAX

	Over	But not over
Single	$43,150	$ 89,560
Married— Filing Jointly	$71,900	$149,250
Married— Filing Separately	$35,950	$113,300
Head of Household	$61,650	$123,790

Filing Requirement One of the benefits of the new tax laws is that many lower-income taxpayers will no longer be required to file a return. You may refer to the following chart to determine if it is necessary for you to file a federal tax return. A return is required if income is at least:

BASE INCOME REQUIRING FILING

Filing Status	1988
Single	$4,950
Head of Household	$6,350
Married Filing Jointly	$8,900
Married Filing Separately	$1,950
Qualifying Widow(er)	$6,950

An individual must file a tax return if her net earnings from self-employment income is $400 or more.

Personal Exemption As a result of the Tax Reform Act of 1986, the personal exemption—the amount you can deduct from your income for each of your dependents—has been raised significantly. In 1987, the personal exemption was $1,900, and it increased to $1,950 in 1988 and $2,000 in 1989. After 1989, the personal exemption will be adjusted for inflation.

The Basic Standard Deduction The zero bracket amount has been replaced by the basic standard deduction. The standard deduction will be taken on the tax return. Unlike the zero bracket amount, the standard deduction is not built into the tax tables, nor does it reduce itemized deductions. Overall, the effect is the same as the zero bracket amount. Your filing status determines the amount of standard deduction you will be allowed. The following chart shows basic standard deductions for 1988.

1988 BASIC STANDARD DEDUCTIONS

Married Filing Jointly	$5,000
Single Taxpayer	$3,000
Married Filing Separately	$2,550
Head of Household	$4,400

The standard deduction is increased for taxpayers over 65 years of age and for the blind. However, the additional personal exemption for these taxpayers has been repealed.

Earned Income Credit The earned income credit assists taxpayers with a child and an adjusted gross income of less than $15,432. The earned income credit has been increased to 14 percent of the first $6,075 of earned income; the maximum refundable credit in 1987 was $851. In 1986, the maxi-

mum refundable credit was $550. The adjusted gross income ceiling has been raised from $11,000 to $15,432. To calculate your earned income credit, if applicable, use the earned income credit worksheet.

Unemployment Income If all goes well, you will be fully employed during the year and not have any unemployment income. If you do, however, you should realize that under the new law all unemployment benefits are fully taxable.

The IRA Deduction Under the old tax law, a taxpayer was allowed to contribute and deduct up to $2,000 a year to his Individual Retirement Account (IRA). The law has been changed so that anyone with an adjusted gross income over $50,000 ($35,000 for a single taxpayer) is no longer able to deduct the IRA contribution. Married taxpayers with an adjusted gross income between $40,000 and $50,000 ($25,000 to $35,000 for single taxpayers) will be able to only partially deduct their IRA contribution.

Repealed Items The Tax Reform Act of 1986 repealed numerous provisions that may affect you as an artist. Income averaging has been eliminated. This method of figuring your taxes by averaging your taxable income over the last three years was frequently used by artists whose income increased dramatically.

The dividend exclusion of $100 for single taxpayers and $200 for married taxpayers filing jointly has also been abolished. So has the 60 percent deduction for long-term capital gains. The deduction for a married couple when both work and the 10 percent investment tax credit for purchases of business equipment have been rescinded.

How to Face an Audit

Approximately two million tax returns a year are selected for audit by the IRS. More than three-fourths of those unfortunate individuals audited are assessed additional tax. Each year the IRS collects more than five billion dollars through the audit process. Obviously, no one wants to face an audit. However, by following a few simple guidelines, you can reduce dramatically your chances of being audited by the IRS. And if you are audited, there are ways of improving your odds of coming out a winner.

How the IRS Selects Individuals to be Audited The best way to avoid triggering an audit is to understand the audit selection process. Overall, less than 2 percent of all tax returns filed are audited. However, as a self-employed artist, you face a greater chance of being audited because of several factors. Generally, self-employed taxpayers are audited more frequently because their deductible business expenses on Schedule C are often challenged by the IRS if they seem out of line with the taxpayer's self-employed income. If you take a home office deduction, as artists often do, then your chances of being audited are also increased. The IRS can audit only a limited number of returns, so it has developed a system for selecting the returns with the highest probability of error and those most likely to result in the greatest amount of additional tax. Usually, then, individuals with large incomes or those who take major deductions are the prime candidates for an invitation from the auditor.

The IRS has two systems it uses for selecting cases for audit. The first is the Taxpayer Compliance Measurement Program, a survey it conducts to determine the average credits, losses, exemptions, and other information it can expect from taxpayers filing returns. The returns used in this survey are selected at random. The main purpose is to encourage compliance with the tax laws and to insure that taxpayers accurately report all income they receive and take only those deductions to which they are entitled. Because returns under this program are selected at random, no taxpayer is safe from being audited. Unlike other kinds of audits where specific items are examined, in this kind of audit, every line on the return must be verified for accuracy.

Data from the Taxpayer Compliance Mea-

surement Program are fed into the IRS computer network and used to establish the taxpayer norms. These norms are then used in another system called the Discriminant Function System (DIF). The DIF computer compares your return with the norms for taxpayers in your income range. Your total positive income is compared with your deductions. If your return differs greatly from the norm, then you are assessed a certain amount of DIF points in each area of variance. The larger the discrepancy, the higher your DIF score. The higher your DIF score, the greater the chances that you will audited. Auditors review the returns with the highest DIF scores, and the ones with the greatest tax increase potential are selected for audit. While most audits are selected by computer, about 25 percent are selected manually. For example, if criminal intent to avoid taxes is suspected, a manual audit may be triggered.

The criteria the IRS uses for determining the DIF score is a more closely guarded secret than the Colonel's special recipe of herbs and spices. However, certain situations are known to trigger audits. Some of the most common reasons for an audit are:

■ *Home Office Deduction.* This deduction is often disallowed. As discussed earlier, taxpayers must meet stringent requirements before this deduction is allowed. Before you decide to take this deduction, you should make sure you meet those requirements. If you do, keep careful records so you can prove your claims if you're audited. (See page 120-123 for more information.)

■ *Losses.* As a self-employed artist, you may have your profit motive challenged by the IRS if you do not show a profit in three of five consecutive years. If you don't meet this requirement, the IRS may consider you to be a hobbyist rather than a professional. Hobby expenses can be deducted only to the extent of the income derived from the activity. What this means is that if your activity is considered to be a hobby by the IRS, then you will not be able to take a loss. (For more information, see page 112.)

■ *Excessive Travel and Entertainment Expenses.*
 ■ *Business Automobile Expenses.*
 ■ *Tax Shelter Activity.*
 ■ *High Income Returns.*
 ■ *Casualty Losses.*
 ■ *Returns Prepared By Questionable Practitioners.*

The Audit Notice If your return is selected for audit, you will receive an invitation to appear before an IRS auditor. Unfortunately, this is one invitation you must accept. Many people believe that if they are not audited within a year after they filed their return, they will not be audited. This is not true. The IRS has three years from the date your return was filed or from the date the return was due to audit your return, although most audits will occur sooner.

You should read your audit letter carefully because it provides you with information that will be useful to you during your interview. The letter explains which items on your return are being questioned. It also explains your basic appeal rights in the event you do not agree with the determination of the auditor. You may also be instructed as to which records you should bring to the audit. If you filed a Schedule C, which you would if you were a self-employed artist, you must bring all supporting ledgers and journals as well as receipts and invoices to the interview. If the appointment date is not convenient, you can call the IRS and make another appointment. If you need more time to prepare for the audit, you may request an extension of time.

Audits may be conducted by correspondence or may occur in your place of business, home, office of your personal representative, or at the IRS office. If you are unable to appear in person, you may request to be audited by mail. You will need to send the IRS a copy of your appointment letter and all documents and records supporting your claim. Be sure to attach a written explanation clearly stating your position on the matter, because in your absence, this information will be all the auditor has to consider in reaching her decision. Conduct an audit by mail only if your case is absolutely clear-cut. Otherwise, I strongly recommend that you appear in person, as your chances of winning an audit are greatly improved.

If you filed jointly, you or your spouse (or both if you choose) may keep the appointment. You may have a qualified person, such as an accountant or attorney, represent you if you are unable to appear, but you must furnish your representative with written authorization to represent you by completing Form 2848.

The Audit Interview Ultimately the result of your audit will depend on your ability to support your position. However, by following certain procedures, you will enhance your chances of a successful outcome.

The best way to be prepared for the audit interview is to bring any records that will substantiate the items being questioned. Have your records organized so that you can easily refer to them and be able to rebut any position the examiner may take that is in opposition to yours. If you are fumbling to locate documents, not only will it look unprofessional, but it will also give the auditor more time to look over your return and try to find other problems. Without records to support your position, you are placing yourself at a distinct disadvantage. The auditor can rule only on what information is made available for examination.

Audits usually last from one to four hours, depending upon the complexity of the case. Always try to cooperate with your agent. If you're hostile, he may think you have something to hide. Answer the questions truthfully, but stick to the subject and don't volunteer any additional information. A slip of the tongue may alert the agent to an error or an unallowable deduction he was not previously aware of. If you have an agent who is not to your liking, you may request that another be assigned to your case. Also, you have the option of terminating the audit at any time if you feel you are being asked questions you cannot answer without professional or legal consultation.

An advantage you have that is often overlooked is that you probably are more familiar with your return than the IRS agent. After all, it's your return, and by the time you are audited, you should know it inside out. The auditor, on the other hand, is frequently assigned your case moments before you walk into her office. She may have hundreds of cases to familiarize herself with, while you have just one.

The Audit Outcome After the audit interview has concluded, the auditor will inform you of his decision. Of the three possible verdicts, two are good. He may agree with your argument and decide that no additional tax is due. Or it is possible that some fact may have been uncovered during the course of the interview that will result in your receiving a refund. The third, and unfortunately most likely, decision is that you owe additional tax.

If the IRS proposes changes that will increase your tax, then you will be notified of your appeal rights. If you agree with the proposed changes, you will be asked to sign the agreement form. If you disagree, you have several options.

First, you may attempt to change the agent's mind. The best way to do that is to present supporting evidence not discussed during the actual audit. If this doesn't work, you may ask to see her supervisor. You should succinctly state why you disagree with the auditor's decision. The supervisor has the power to overturn the decision or offer a compromise if your arguments are persuasive.

If the situation is still not resolved to your satisfaction, then you have thirty days to appeal. You may appeal through the IRS or through the courts. In most instances, it is advantageous to appeal through IRS channels first. Appeals through the court system can be costly. In most cases, you will be required to hire an attorney or other qualified person to represent you. Another advantage of appealing through the IRS is that if you lose, you can still appeal through the courts.

Appeals Through the IRS To appeal through IRS channels, write the IRS District Director requesting a conference in the Appeals Office. If the increase in tax is greater than $2,500, then you will need to file a written protest with the Regional Director of Appeals. You may represent yourself or be represented by a qualified person at the hearing. The district conferee, who has the authority to reverse any previous rulings, will consider your argument. You should restate your case and present any documentation supporting your position. When the hearing is over, the district conferee will reach a decision. In most cases, the IRS is not any more eager to go to tax court than you are, so there's a good possibility of compromise. At this stage, you must consider if further appeals will be more costly than the amount being disputed.

Appeals Through the Courts If you cannot reach an agreement with the IRS, you may appeal your case to the United States Tax Court, the United States Claims Court, or the United States District Court. Unless the disputed amount is extremely large, your case can be handled in the Small Claims Division. Once the case has reached the courts, you should rely solely on the advice of your attorney.

COMMONLY ASKED QUESTIONS: TAXES

Q. *I donated five wildlife paintings to the Natural History Museum. How should I report this on my tax return?*

A. If you donate your art to a qualified organization, such as a museum, then you generally may deduct the fair market value of the donation at the time of the contribution. The fair market value is the price at which property would change hands between a willing buyer and a willing seller. The IRS keeps close tabs on such donations, so be sure not to overvalue your work or you may be subject to a stiff penalty.

Q. *I bartered five watercolors for a bookcase. How do I report this?*

A. You must report the fair market value of property received in bartering, in this case the bookcase, on Schedule C.

Q. *Over the last five years, I have shown my work in several galleries and have completed several commissions. However, I did not realize a profit in three of those years. I don't classify myself as a hobbyist. Does the IRS?*

A. The IRS considers you a hobbyist unless you have shown a profit in at least three of the last five years. If you file as a business and are audited, you must present convincing evidence of your intention to make a profit. Factors considered by the IRS to demonstrate your profit motive include the manner in which you conduct your business, your expertise as an artist, the amount of time and effort you put into your art, expectation of future profits, success in similar ventures, your history of profit and losses, the amount of occasional profits, your financial status, and elements of personal pleasure or recreation.

Q. *I do both fine art and illustration/design. Should I keep separate records?*

A. I recommend that you keep separate records for your fine art and illustration/design income. The more detailed the recordkeeping, the better. A really good recordkeeping system will allow you to reconstruct all your sources of income and deductions at tax time, when it really matters.

Q. *I use a van to deliver my artwork around the area and to transport it to various art shows throughout several states. I also use the van on family vacations. Can I deduct my expenses in using the van?*

A. You are permitted to deduct any expenses that are related to your profession, but not personal expenses. Expenses incurred while using your van to deliver artwork would be deductible, while personal use of the van, such as taking it on a vacation, would not qualify as a deductible expense. It's important to maintain separate records for the business and personal use of your motor vehicle.

Q. *I took a trip to New York to visit the galleries and museums. Can I deduct my trip expenses, since this was research for my work?*

A. Under the new tax laws, travel done exclusively for educational value is not deductible. However, if travel is necessary to conduct research where it cannot be done elsewhere, then it is deductible.

Q. *If I choose to buy a Mercedes 450 SL to deliver jobs, can it be considered a business expense, or a portion of it? I'm both a freelancer and an art director.*

A. The IRS maintains its right to disallow excessive business expenses. What constitutes an excessive business expense is open to interpretation, but allowable business expenses are those necessary for conducting your business. Since Mercedes delivery vans are at a premium, I suggest that you acquire less extravagant means of transportation if you want to deduct it.

Q. *Do I have to worry about collecting sales tax on works sold at art shows?*

A. Most states require that you charge sales tax on art sold at art shows. First, register with the state sales tax department, which will give you a sales permit and a resale number plus the appropriate forms. Record all sales taxes on your sales invoices and in your bookkeeping journals. Then, every three months, total the taxes collected and send the check, with the return marked with your resale number, to the state sales tax department. For art shows held out of state, ask the sales tax department of that state to provide whatever forms it requires.

Q. *My studio is located in my home and is used regularly and exclusively as my principal place of business. I did not make a profit on my artwork last year. Can I still claim the home office deduction?*

A. You are not allowed to use your home office deduction to produce a net loss. You can deduct only home office expenses equal to the net profit from the sale of your artwork. Deductions that exceed the limit may be carried forward to later years.

EASY REFERENCE CHECKLISTS: TAXES

Good recordkeeping starts with separating business and personal items.

Business items include:
- ☐ Income from the sale of your work
- ☐ Expenses you generate running your business, such as overhead
- ☐ Expenses you incur with creating your work, such as paint or canvas
- ☐ Expenses you incur in servicing your accounts, such as gasoline and parking fees

Some expenses to record:
- ☐ Supplies, tools, and equipment
- ☐ Dues, publication subscriptions, books
- ☐ Travel
- ☐ Business meals and entertainment
- ☐ Office supplies and postage
- ☐ Commissions to other artists
- ☐ Conferences, continuing education, training

Some expenses that are 100 percent deductible are:
- ☐ Subscriptions to trade journals
- ☐ Professional dues
- ☐ Home office expenses
- ☐ Commissions to art representatives or agents
- ☐ Costs of printing brochures and self-promotional material
- ☐ Mailing and freight expenses
- ☐ Insurance
- ☐ Jury fees and entry fees

Some expenses that are 80 percent deductible are:
- ☐ Business meals
- ☐ Entertainment of clients
- ☐ Tips
- ☐ Cover charges

Records to keep:
- [ ] Invoices
- [ ] Vouchers
- [ ] Bills
- [ ] Receipts for expenditures and sales
- [ ] Register tapes
- [ ] Canceled checks
- [ ] Deposit slips
- [ ] Expense diary entries

Make sure that all records show:
- [ ] Who the buyer or seller is
- [ ] What the item was purchased for
- [ ] When the transaction took place
- [ ] Where the transaction took place
- [ ] The purpose of the transaction, and if you have given it a name or number

Two methods of accounting:
- [ ] Cash method records income when it is received and expenses when they are paid.
- [ ] Accrual method records income when it is earned, not received, and expenses when they are incurred. If you have a large inventory, this is the best method.

Schedules you may have to file in addition to your 1040:
- [ ] Schedule A, itemized deductions
- [ ] Schedule B, if you receive more than $400 in interest or dividend income
- [ ] Schedule C, to determine profit or loss from your business
- [ ] Schedule SE, to calculate Social Security tax liability for the year
- [ ] Schedule D, to report capital gains and losses
- [ ] Schedule E, to report supplemental income, such as royalties
- [ ] Form 4562, to calculate depreciation of equipment

Tax publications helpful to artists:
- [ ] 334 Tax Guide for Small Business
- [ ] 463 Travel, Entertainment and Gift Expenses
- [ ] 505 Tax Withholding and Estimated Tax
- [ ] 525 Taxable and Nontaxable Income
- [ ] 533 Self-Employment Tax
- [ ] 535 Business Expenses
- [ ] 538 Accounting Periods and Methods
- [ ] 587 Business Use of Your Home
- [ ] 910 Guide to Free Tax Services
- [ ] 917 Business Use of Car

VOLUNTEER LAWYERS FOR THE ARTS

UNITED STATES

California

San Diego Lawyers for the Arts
1205 Prospect St.
Suite 400
La Jolla CA 92037
619/454-9696
Peter Karlen, Director

California Lawyers for the Arts (CALA)
For Mason Center, Building C
San Francisco CA 94123
415/775-7200
Alma Robinson, Esq.

Colorado

Colorado Lawyers for the Arts (COLA)
P.O. Box 300428
Denver CO 80203
303/830-0379
K. Holly Bennett, Esq.

Connecticut

Connecticut Volunteer Lawyers for the Arts (CTVLA)
Connecticut Commission on the Arts
190 Trumbull St.
Hartford CT 06103-2206
Brian J. Anderson, Legislative Liaison

District of Columbia

District of Columbia Lawyers Committee for the Arts/Volunteer Lawyers for the Arts, D.C.
918 Sixteenth St. NW, Suite 503
Washington DC 20006
202/429-0229
Joshua Kaufman, Esq.

Florida

Volunteer Lawyers and Accountant for the Arts Program
Pinellas County Arts Council
400 Pierce Blvd.
Clearwater FL 33516
813/462-3327
Peggy MacLeod, Executive Director

Broward Arts Council
100 South Andrews Ave.
Fort Lauderdale FL 33301
305/357-7457
Mary A. Becht, Director

Business Volunteers for the Arts/Miami (BVA)
%Greater Miami Chamber of Commerce
1601 Biscayne Boulevard
Miami FL 33132
305/350-7700
Dr. Susan Wallace-Reiling, Executive Director

Georgia

Georgia Volunteer Lawyers for the Arts (GVLA)
P.O. Box 1131
Atlanta GA 30301-1131
404/586-4945
Glenn Chitlik, Program Director

Illinois

Lawyers for the Creative Arts (LCA)
623 South Wabash Avenue, Suite 300-N
Chicago IL 60605
312/427-1800
Joan Kurlen, Esq., Executive Director

Iowa

Volunteer Lawyers for the Arts Committee
Cedar Rapids/Marion Arts Council
424 First Ave. N.E., P.O. Drawer 4860
Cedar Rapids IA 52407
319/398-5322
Elizabeth A. Zeidel, Executive Director

Kentucky

Lexington Council of the Arts
161 N. Mill St.
Lexington KY 40507
607/255-2951
Dee Peretz, Executive Director

Community Arts Council
609 W. Main St.
Louisville KY 40202
502/582-1821
Baylor Landrum, Director of External Affairs

Louisiana

Louisiana Volunteer Lawyers for the Arts
(LVLA)
%Arts Council of New Orleans
WTC Building, Suite 936
2 Canal St.
New Orleans LA 70130
504/523-1465
Ginny Lee McMurray, Assistant Director

Maine

Maine Volunteer Lawyers for the Arts
Maine Commission on the Arts
55 Capitol St.
State House Station 25
Augusta ME 04333
207/289-2724
Daniel T. Crocker, Management Analyst

Maryland

Maryland Lawyers for the Arts
%University of Baltimore School of Law
1420 North Charles St.
Baltimore MD 21201
301/685-0600
Kirk Kolodner, Esq., Executive Director

Massachusetts

The Arts Extension Service (AES)
Division of Continuing Education
University of Massachusetts
Amherst MA 01003
413/545-2360
Craig Dreeszen, Education Coordinator

Lawyers and Accountants for the Arts
The Artists Foundation, Inc.
110 Broad St.
Boston MA 02169
617/482-8100
Ron P. Rothman, Executive Director

Minnesota

Minnesota Volunteer Lawyers for the Arts
100 South Fifth St., Suite 1500
Minneapolis MN 55402
612/337-1500
Fred Rosenblatt, Esq., President

Missouri

St. Louis Volunteer Lawyers and Accountant
for the Arts (SLVAA)
%St. Louis Regional Arts Commission
329 N. Euclid Ave.
St. Louis MO 63108
314/361-7686
Marvin Nodiff, Esq., President

Montana

Montana Volunteer Lawyers for the Arts
P.O. Box 8687
Missoula MT 69807
406/721-1835
Joan Jonkel, Esq.

New Jersey

Volunteer Lawyers for the Arts of New Jersey
36 W. Lafayette St.
Trenton NJ 08608
609/695-6422
Judith Trachtenberg, Esq., Director

New York

Volunteer Lawyers for the Arts Program
Albany League of Arts
19 Clinton Ave.
Albany NY 12207
518/449-5380
Maureen Salkin, Executive Director

Arts Council in Buffalo and Erie County
700 Main St.
Buffalo NY 14202
716/856-7520
Janet Newcomb, Program Coordinator

Huntington Arts Council, Inc.
213 Main St.
Huntington NY 11743
516/271-8423
Cindy Kiebitz, Executive Director

Volunteer Lawyers for the Arts (VLA)
1285 Avenue of the Americas
Third Floor
New York NY 10019
212/977-9270
Jennifer Moyer, Executive Director

Dutchess County Arts Council
39 Market St.
Poughkeepsie NY 12601
914/454-3222
Judith M. Levine, Executive Director

North Carolina

North Carolina Volunteer Lawyers for the Arts
P.O. Box 590
Raleigh NC 27602
919/890-3195

Ohio

Cincinnati Lawyers for the Arts
2500 Central Trust Center
201 E. Fifth St.
Cincinnati OH 45202
513/651-6746
Roger A. Gilcrest, Director

Volunteer Lawyers and Accountants for the Arts Program
%Cleveland Bar Association
Mall Building
118 St. Clair Ave.
Cleveland OH 44114
216/696-3525
Susan Stevens Jaros, Chairman

Arnold Gottlieb
421 N. Michigan St.
Suite D
Toledo OH 43624
419/243-3125

Pennsylvania

Philadelphia Volunteer Lawyers for the Arts
251 South 18th St.
Philadelphia PA 19103
215/545-3385
Dorothy R.B. Manou, Executive Director

Rhode Island

Ocean State Lawyers for the Arts
96 Sachem Rd.
Narrangansett RI 02882
401/789-5686
David M. Spatt, Esq., Director

South Carolina

South Carolina Lawyers for the Arts
P.O. Box 10023
Greenville SC 29603
803/232-6970
C. Diana Smock, Esq., Legal Director

Tennessee

Tennessee Arts Commission
320 Sixth Ave. N.
Nashville TN 37219
Bennett Tarleton

Texas

Austin Lawyers and Accountants for the Arts
P.O. Box 2577
Austin TX 78768
512/476-7573
Robert M. Sweeney, Executive Director

Texas Accountants and Lawyers for the Arts
1540 Sul Rose
Houston TX 77006
713/526-4876
Nan Harris, Attorney
Sarah Roady, Executive Director

Utah

Utah Lawyers for the Arts
50 South Main, Suite 900
Salt Lake City UT 84144
801/521-5800
Caludette Harris, Secretary

Washington

Washington Volunteer Lawyers for the Arts
428 Joseph Vance Building
1402 Third Ave.
Seattle WA 98101
206/223-0502
Stephanie Johnson O'Day, Acting Director

CANADA

Canadian Artists' Representation Ontario
(CARO)
345-67 Mowat Avenue
Toronto Ontario M6K3E3
Canada
416/534-8218

INDEX

Other Art Books from North Light

Graphics/Business of Art

Airbrush Artist's Library (3 in series) $12.95 cloth)

Airbrush Techniques Workbooks (8 in series) $9.95 each

Airbrushing the Human Form, by Paul Berman $27.95 (cloth)

The Art & Craft of Greeting Cards, by Susan Evarts $15.95 (paper)

The Artist's Friendly Legal Guide, by Conner, Karlen, Perwin, & Spatt $15.95 (paper)

Artist's Market: Where & How to Sell Your Graphic Art (Annual Directory) $18.95 (cloth)

Basic Graphic Design & Paste-Up, by Jack Warren $12.95 (paper)

Complete Airbrush & Photoretouching Manual, by Peter Owen & John Sutcliffe $23.95 (cloth)

The Complete Guide to Greeting Card Design & Illustration, by Eva Szela $27.95 (cloth)

Color Harmony: A Guide to Creative Color Combinations, by Hideaki Chijiiwa $15.95 (paper)

Creative Ad Design & Illustration, by Dick Ward $32.95 (cloth)

Creative Typography, by Liz McQuiston $27.95 (cloth)

Design Rendering Techniques, by Dick Powell $29.95 (cloth)

Dynamic Airbrush, by David Miller & James Effler $29.95 (cloth)

Fashion Illustration Workbooks (4 in series) $8.95 each

Fantasy Art, by Bruce Robertson $24.95 (cloth)

Getting It Printed, by Beach, Shepro & Russon $29.50 (paper)

The Graphic Arts Studio Manual, by Bert Braham $22.95 (cloth)

The Graphic Artist's Guide to Marketing & Self-Promotion, by Sally Prince Davis $15.95 (paper)

Graphic Tools & Techniques, by Laing & Saunders-Davies $24.95 (cloth)

Graphics Handbook, by Howard Munce $13.95 (paper)

How to Design Trademarks & Logos, by Murphy & Row $24.95 (cloth)

How to Draw & Sell Cartoons, by Ross Thomson & Bill Hewison $15.95 (cloth)

How to Draw & Sell Comic Strips, by Alan McKenzie $18.95 (cloth)

How to Draw Charts & Diagrams, by Bruce Robertson $24.95 (cloth)

How to Understand & Use Design & Layout, by Alan Swann $22.95 (cloth)

How to Write and Illustrate Children's Books, edited by Treld Pelkey Bicknell and Felicity Trotman, $22.50 (cloth)

Illustration & Drawing: Styles & Techniques, by Terry Presnall $22.95 (cloth)

Marker Rendering Techniques, by Dick Powell & Patricia Monahan $32.95 (cloth)

Marker Techniques Workbooks (4 in series) $9.95 each

The North Light Art Competition Handbook, by John M. Angelini $9.95 (paper)

North Light Dictionary of Art Terms, by Margy Lee Elspass $10.95 (paper)

Preparing Your Design for Print, by Lynn John $27.95 (cloth)

Presentation Techniques for the Graphic Artist, by Jenny Mulherin $24.95 (cloth)

Print Production Handbook, by David Bann $14.95 (cloth)

Studio Secrets for the Graphic Artist, by Graham et al $27.50 (cloth)

Type: Design, Color, Character & Use, by Michael Beaumont $24.95 (cloth)

Using Type Right, by Philip Brady $18.95 (paper)

Watercolor

Basic Watercolor Painting, by Judith Campbell-Reed $16.95 (paper)

Capturing Mood in Watercolor, by Phil Austin, $26.95 (cloth)

Chinese Watercolor Painting: The Four Seasons, by Leslie Tseng-Tseng Yu $24.95 (paper)

Getting Started in Watercolor, by John Blockley $19.95 (paper)

Make Your Watercolors Sing, by LaVere Hutchings $22.95 (cloth)

Painting Flowers with Watercolor, by Ethel Todd George $17.95 (paper)

Painting Nature's Details in Watercolor, by Cathy Johnson $24.95 (cloth)

Watercolor Energies, by Frank Webb $17.95 (paper)

Watercolor Fast & Loose, by Ron Ranson $21.95 (cloth)

Watercolor for All Seasons, by Elaine and Murray Wentworth $21.95 (cloth)

Watercolor Interpretations, by John Blockley $19.95 (paper)

Watercolor Options, by Ray Loos $22.50 (cloth)

Watercolor Painter's Solution Book, by Angela Gair $24.95 (cloth)

Watercolor Painting on Location, by El Meyer $19.95 (cloth)

Watercolor—The Creative Experience, by Barbara Nechis $16.95 (paper)

Watercolor Tricks & Techniques, by Cathy Johnson $24.95 (cloth)

Watercolor Workbook, by Bud Biggs & Lois Marshall $18.95 (paper)

Watercolor: You Can Do It!, by Tony

Couch $25.95 (cloth)
Wet Watercolor, by Wilfred Ball $24.95 (cloth)

Watercolor Videos

Watercolor Fast & Loose, with Ron Ranson $29.95 (VHS or Beta)
Watercolor Pure & Simple, with Ron Ranson $29.95 (VHS or Beta)

Mixed Media

The Art of Scratchboard, by Cecile Curtis $21.95 (cloth)
Calligraphy Workbooks (4 in series) $7.95 each
Catching Light in Your Paintings, by Charles Sovek $18.95 (paper)
Colored Pencil Drawing Techniques, by Iain Hutton-Jamieson $23.95 (cloth)
Complete Guide to Fashion Illustration, by Colin Barnes $32.95 (cloth)
Drawing & Painting with Ink, by Fritz Henning $24.95 (cloth)
Drawing By Sea & River, by John Croney $14.95 (cloth)
Drawing for Pleasure, edited by Peter D. Johnson $15.95 (paper)
Drawing Workbooks (4 in series) $8.95 each
Encyclopaedia of Drawing, by Clive Ashwin $22.50 (cloth)
Exploring Color, by Nita Leland $26.95 (cloth)
The Figure, edited by Walt Reed $15.95 (paper)
Keys to Drawing, by Bert Dodson $21.95 (cloth)
Light: How to See It, How to Paint It, by Lucy Willis $24.95 (cloth)
Landscape Painting, by Patricia Monahan $19.95 (cloth)
Make Your Own Picture Frames, by Jenny Rodwell $12.95 (paper)
Mixing Color, by Jeremy Galton $24.95 (cloth)
The North Light Handbook of Artist's

Materials, by Ian Hebblewhite $24.95 (cloth)
The North Light Illustrated Book of Painting Techniques, by Elizabeth Tate $26.95 (cloth)
Oil Painting: A Direct Approach, by Joyce Pike $26.95 (cloth)
On Drawing and Painting, by Paul Landry $15.95 (cloth)
Painting & Drawing Boats, by Moira Huntley $16.95 (paper)
Painting Birds & Animals, by Patricia Monahan $21.95 (cloth)
Painting in Oils, edited by Michael Bowers $18.95 (cloth)
Painting Nature, by Franklin Jones $17.95 (paper)
Painting Murals, by Patricia Seligman $24.95 (cloth)
Painting Portraits, by Jenny Rodwell $21.95 (cloth)
Painting Seascapes in Sharp Focus, by Lin Seslar $24.95 (cloth)
Painting with Acrylics, by Jenny Rodwell $19.95 (cloth)
Painting with Oils, by Patricia Monahan $19.95 (cloth)
Painting with Pastels, edited by Peter D. Johnson $16.95 (paper)
Pastel Painting Techniques, by Guy Roddon $24.95 (cloth)
The Pencil, by Paul Calle $16.95 (paper)
People Painting Scrapbook, by J. Everett Draper $26.95 (cloth)
Perspective in Art, by Michael Woods $13.95 (paper)
Photographing Your Artwork, by Russell Hart $15.95 (paper)
Putting People in Your Paintings, by J. Everett Draper $22.50 (cloth)
The Techniques of Wood Sculpture, by David Orchard $14.95 (cloth)
Tonal Values: How to See Them, How to Paint Them, by Angela Gair $24.95 (cloth)
You Can Learn Lettering & Calligraphy, by Gail & Christopher Lawther $15.95 (cloth)